THE STORY OF
STAMFORD

MARTIN SMITH

D1586222

The Story of

'TAMFORD

ISBN

HARDBACK:
1 899141 00 6
PAPERBACK:
1 899141 22 7

PUBLISHED *by*

MARTIN SMITH
in association with
WALKER'S
BOOKS LTD.
Stamford

DISTRIBUTED *by*

MARTIN SMITH
3 Stanley Street
Stamford, Lincs
PE9 1EX
01780 481236

**TYPESET
& DESIGNED** *by*

MARTIN SMITH
in Baskerville

**PRINTED
& BOUND** *by*

The ALDEN PRESS
Oxford

TITLE PAGE
Section of Buck's *South
Prospect of Stamford*, 1743

CONTENTS

CHRONOLOGY OF EVENTS

C1 Roman Ermine Street built

C9 Saxon enclosure possibly founded in St Peter's area

Late **C9** Danes build a borough north of River Welland

918 Edward the Elder takes control of Stamford and builds southern borough

Early **C10** Growth of pottery industry

c. **950s** Stamford becomes one of the 5 Boroughs of Danelaw. An important mint is established in the town

Early **C11** Lincolnshire is formed. Stamford loses territory to Lincoln. Peterborough Abbey gains control of St Martin's

1066 Norman Conquest

1068 Norman Castle built at Stamford

1086 Stamford surveyed in Domesday

Early **C12** St Leonard's Priory built

1153 Stamford Castle besieged and captured by Henry of Anjou, later Henry II

c. **1155** St Michael's Nunnery founded

1156 Henry II gives control of Stamford borough to Richard du Hommet

mid **C12** Decline of pottery industry. Growth of trade in wool, cloth and grain. Mid-Lent fair an event of international importance. Town has 14 churches

c. **1170** River Trent bridged at Newark. Great North Road passes through Stamford

1189 Following attacks, Jews take refuge in castle

1194 Stamford allowed to stage tournaments

1204 William de Warenne is given control of Stamford borough

Early **C13** All 4 orders of friars settle in Stamford

Mid **C13** With a population of *c.*5,000, Stamford is one of the largest towns in England.

1240 Stamford borough reverts to king after death of William de Warenne

1254 Barons' War begins

1265 Stamford borough given to John de Warenne

1274-5 *Hundred Rolls* reveal Warenne's aggressive lordship

1290 Edward I expels Jews from England

1313 Warenne gives town some degree of self-government

1338 Hundred Years' War with France begins

Early **C14** Town in decline as wool sales drop and cloth trade moves elsewhere

1333-5 Attempt by Oxford students and masters to set up rival university in Stamford

1347 John de Warenne dies

1349 Black Death hits Stamford

1363 Edmund Langley, later Duke of York, given control of Stamford borough

1381 Peasants' Revolt

Mid **C15** Rich patrons begin rebuilding programme of Stamford's main churches. Smaller churches begin to close

1452 Stamford involved in Yorkist rising

1461 Stamford sacked in Wars of the Roses

1462 Stamford's Charter of Incorporation

1470 Battle of Losecoat Field

1475 Foundation of Browne's Hospital

1481 2nd Charter of Incorporation

1520 William Cecil born

1536/38 Dissolution of the monasteries. Smaller churches in the town are shut

1536 Lincolnshire's Pilgrimage of Grace

1555-87 Building of Burghley House

1558-9 William Cecil becomes Secretary of State. Elizabeth I's religious settlement. Cecil helps build new Town Hall at Stamford

Mid **C16** William Cecil gains control of Stamford. Town in severe economic hardship

1572 William Cecil made Lord Burghley and Lord Treasurer

1587 Execution of Mary Queen of Scots at Fotheringhay

1598 Cecil dies; a tomb is erected in St Martin's. Thomas, his eldest son, inherits Burghley

Early **C17** Wothorpe House built by Thomas Cecil

1603 Richard Norris sets up bellfounding business

1604 Plague hits Stamford

1605 Thomas Cecil made 1st Earl of Exeter

1628 Manor of Stamford passes to Grey family, Earls of Stamford

1642 Outbreak of Civil War

1643 Siege of Burghley House

1646 King Charles hides at Stamford

1648 Royalist uprising at Stamford

1649 Execution of Charles I

1660 Restoration of monarchy

1664 Opening of Welland Navigation Canal

CHRONOLOGY OF EVENTS

1674 First Classical-style house built in Stamford

1680s Bertie family of Grimsthorpe and Uffington dominate local politics

1688 Glorious Revolution: William III and Mary take the throne

1698 Political alliance formed between Cecils and Berties. Now united as Tories they each take one Stamford seat

*Late***C17** The town emerges as a centre for both the malting and coaching trades

1704 Cassandra King is the last person to be tried and hanged at Stamford

1712 Publication of *Stamford Mercury*

1717 Racecourse opens on Wittering Heath

1724 George Hotel rebuilt

1727 Stamford gets one of the first assembly rooms in the country

*mid***C18** Prosperity from the Great North Road encourages house building

1734 Cecils manipulate election. Their electoral supremacy is not challenged again until 1809

1730s William Stukeley, famous antiquarian, is Rector of All Saints' Church

1768 Theatre opened

1776 New Town Hall built

1788 Corporation and Cecils try to stop bull running festival

1780s Large-scale town rebuilding programme by 9th Earl of Exeter

1809 Contested election. Death of Daniel Lambert

1810 Stamford Hotel begun by Noel family as centre of electoral opposition to Cecils

1830 Charles Tennyson only just fails to be elected

1831 Charles Tennyson beats Cecil candidate at the reform election

1832 Reform Act actually strengthens Cecil's political position. Tennyson stands down

1835 Stamford Corporation is reformed

1839 Last bull-running

1844 Queen Victoria visits Burghley

1846 Main railway line from London to North-East to pass through Peterborough

1848 Midland railway line opened connecting Stamford with Peterborough and Leicester

1850s End of coaching trade

1855 Stamford East station opened with lines to Essendine and later Wansford

1867 Second Reform Act leaves town with only 1 MP and doubles the number of voters

1870s Theatre and racecourse close. Schools improved

1875 Enclosure of the northern fields allows town to expand

1880 Liberal MP elected

1886 Blackstones move to Ryhall Road site and start building oil engines

1889 Stamford put under Kesteven County Council

1896 Stamford Football Club formed

1903 Pick Motor Company becomes one of the largest car manufacturers in East Midlands

1900-10 Population increasing for first time in 50 years

1910 Picturedrome cinema opens

1914 Stamford industry helps war effort

1921 First council houses built

1920s Economic depression

1940 Bomb lands in St Leonard's Street

1954 1,000th council house built

1960 A1 bypass opened

1967 Stamford becomes first conservation area in England

1972 High Street pedestrianised

1974 Stamford loses its borough status. Melbourne's Brewery closes

1980s Stamford increasingly becomes a tourist and retirement town

1993 Mirrlees Blackstone ceases all engine production in Stamford. Filming of BBC's *Middlemarch*

1994 East-west bypass dropped by government. Stamford is represented by the Labour Party for the first time (European Parliament)

FOREWORD

Stamford is a town which has always encouraged superlatives. Celia Fiennes, the late 17th-century traveller, said Stamford is 'as fine a built town all of stone as may be seen'. Sir Walter Scott apparently doffed his hat to the view up to St Mary's Church, claiming it was the finest sight on the road between London and Edinburgh. John Betjeman called Stamford 'England's best town'. Lady Wedgewood, writing in 1936, said 'Among stone-built towns there may be some that equal, none I think that surpass Stamford and, since here the Welland leaves the freestone country to enter on the vagaries of a Fen river, it certainly chooses the supreme, architectural moment.' Pevsner says 'The climax [of Lincolnshire] in terms of historical as well as architectural significance, is... the town of Stamford, the English country market town *par excellence*'. W. G. Hoskins, the famous 1950s historian, said:

> If there is a more beautiful town in the whole of England I have yet to see it. The view of Stamford from the water-meadows on a fine June evening, about a quarter to half a mile upstream, is one of the finest sights that England has to show. The western sunlight catches the grey limestone walls and turns them to gold. It falls on towers and spires and flowing water, on the warm brown roofs of Collyweston slates, and on the dark mass of the Burghley woods behind. The hipped and mansard roofs of the town rise from the edge of the river above the flashing willows, tier upon tier, to the spire of All Saints, and the towers of St Martin's, St John's, and St Michael's, and, above them all, to the noble tower and spire of St Mary's, the central jewel in the crown of Stamford...
>
> *[East Midlands and the Peak*, ed. G. Grigson (London, 1951)]

In 1993, BBC television used Stamford as the setting for George Eliot's *Middlemarch* drama. The producer, Louis Marks, said 'When we were planning the programme we presumed we would have to film all over the country - a street here, a square there, a house somewhere else. But then our researchers came back and told us they had found this marvellous town that had everything. So I went up to Lincolnshire, took one look and I knew they were right. Stamford is beautiful, extraordinary; it is absolutely stunning'.

Stamford is set in gently rolling countryside just west of the fen edge. This is a landscape of woods and agricultural land punctuated by delightful stone villages and aristocratic estates. To again quote W. G. Hoskins:

> In the country, the villages of the Stone Belt - built in the golden ironstone or the sheep-grey oolitic limestone - are some of them superb, not to be outdone anywhere in England. Such are Collyweston and Duddington, in northern Northamptonshire, and Clipsham, Caldecott, and Preston, to name only three in Rutland, where nearly every village is worth exploring...

This book is the latest in a long tradition of Stamford histories and guides beginning with Richard Butcher's *The Survey and the Antiquities of the Towne of Stamford* published in 1646. Hopefully it is the most comprehensive and accurate. The story of the town unfolds through 1,000 years of history. Local events are always linked into national history, particularly in the pre-Conquest period, the Wars of the Roses, the Reformation and Civil War. As the town becomes increasingly provincial, so the national references decline. Combined with the main text is a selective Gazetteer to the buildings and sites of Stamford and the surrounding area.

ACKNOWLEDGEMENTS

I would like to thank Shaun Tyas of Paul Watkins Publishing for all his help and advice and for publishing my other books. I thank John Smith, Curator of Stamford Museum, for giving up so much of his precious time to comment on the text. His contribution has been invaluable. I also thank Dave Roffe and Christine Mahany for guiding me through the early history of the town. I thank Anne Wilkins for correcting my grammar, Graham Dale for reading the text and Barry Ketchum of Staniland booksellers for his comments. I thank Philip Riley for his thorough proof-reading. I thank Mike Key of Stamford Museum for his comments on the text and Stamford Museum for permission to use some of their photographs. I thank Frances Balam for all her photographic work and the excellent cover photograph. I thank Stamford Fire Brigade for allowing us to photograph from their tower. I also thank Stamford Library and the Town Hall. Finally, I gratefully acknowledge the financial support of my parents, Newage International and South Kesteven District Council.

DANELAW

Above: *11th century tower at Barnack, 4 miles south-east of Stamford*

LATE IN eighth-century Britain there appeared 'dire portents... immense whirlwinds... flashes of lightning... and fiery dragons... flying in the air'. The Viking raids had begun. What followed was a century of plundering, conquest and settlement by Norwegians and Danes, known collectively as *Vikings*, or 'pirates', by their enemies. The Norwegians sailed around the north of Scotland to the Western Isles and Ireland, while the Danes concentrated on England. In 865, the Danish 'Great Army', led by Halfdan and Ivar the Boneless, landed in East Anglia; by 871 the Danes were in control of all eastern England as far as Northumbria and Alfred the Great of Wessex was forced to buy them off to avoid invasion of his south-western Kingdom. In the middle Kingdom of Mercia, the Danes became involved in local politics, siding with a rival dynasty to expel King Burgred. Following the failure of a Danish attack on Wessex in 878, England was bisected by a border running along the old Roman Watling Street from London to Chester.

The Danes began consolidating their northern and eastern territories. Deep in eastern Mercia, beyond the great forests of Rutland and on the edge of the marshy fens, northern Danes (perhaps from the York area) might have encountered a small Saxon settlement on a hill by the River Welland. The site was attractive. The undulating landscape of the area, formed by a rich belt of Jurassic limestone, offered good terrain for travellers. The area was a place for passing through, and this characteristic dominated the history of the town that later grew up here: Stamford was destined to be a town determined by its routes of communication. Early man had travelled through here along ancient trackways, north to settlements along the River Trent and south into East Anglia. An early track route, now known as the Jurassic Way, followed the limestone belt across England from Dorset, through the Midlands, to the Humber and beyond. When the Romans arrived in the first century BC they had built their main road from London to York through this corridor. Ermine Street crossed the valley of the River Welland about half a mile west of the present town; the site of the stone-paved ford is still visible today and the line of the road north is defined by the modern streets of Water Furlong and Roman Bank. The Anglo-Saxon place-name, *Stamford*, is Old English and derives either from the Roman 'stone ford' or the later ford just east of the Town Bridge.

The Welland valley itself was an important area of early settlement. Gravel terraces in the fens were densely populated from prehistoric times. There were extensive settlements in the Tallington and Market Deeping area, and a Bronze Age site was discovered near the river about one mile east

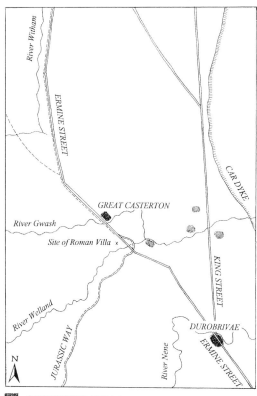

ROMAN SETTLEMENT *(selected sites)*
BRONZE AGE SETTLEMENT *(selected sites)*

of Stamford. But the Romans ignored the Welland, building on the rivers Nene and Gwash instead. Their town of *Durobrivae*, ten miles south on the River Nene near the village of Water Newton, became a famous pottery centre, while on the River Gwash, two miles north of the Welland, a small town and military camp was set up at what is now Great Casterton where a defensive ditch can still be seen. Roman villas and farms dotted the sides of the Welland valley but as far as we know no major development occurred.

So what was the settlement that the Danes found? Excavations of the castle site in Stamford during the 1970s uncovered a small section of the defensive ditches of what was possibly a late ninth-century enclosure. These ditches might have protected an early type of fortified house, occupied by a lord, perhaps consisting of a timber hall and outbuildings; a good example has been found at Goltho just east of Lincoln. The enclosure belonged to the ancient Mercian royal estate of *Roteland* or Rutland which at that time included the modern St Peter's area of Stamford. From the tenth century or earlier, this estate was part of the dowry of the Mercian queens and was endowed with an area of agricultural land (called Portland after the Conquest) which lay to the west of Ermine Street. The siting of the estate was advantageous. It stood on a defensible hill just above the route to an early river crossing, which probably ran down modern Wothorpe Road, across the water meadows and up a stream valley now occupied by Castle Dyke. A church was often founded adjacent to an enclosure to serve the religious needs of the lord. It is probable that St Peter's Church, which stood on the grassy hill by the modern bus station, was the estate church and so the 'mother'

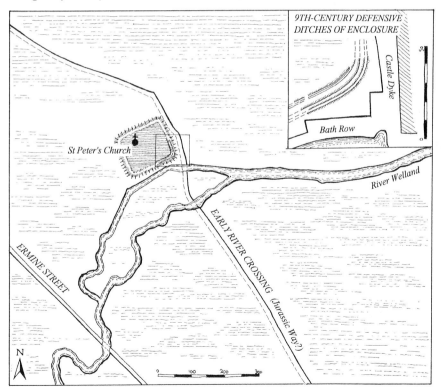

Opposite: *Early roads and settlements in the Stamford area. The Car Dyke is a Roman fenland drainage channel*
Above: *Conjectured extent of late 9th century Anglo-Saxon settlement. Inset shows detail of excavated ditches*

THE STORY OF STAMFORD

church of Stamford. Around the enclosure and church a community might have developed; small timber houses, perhaps similar to those found at Maxey five miles to the east, could have clustered around the core.

The advantages of settlement here were obvious and the Danes were quick to recognise this. The river offered easy transport through the fens to the Wash and the North Sea and the spot was the narrowest and best defensible site along the valley. The early river crossings were testimony to this and in turn gave excellent inland communications along major track routes. The Danes built a borough east of the earlier enclosure on terraces north of the narrowest point in the river valley. The present High Street formed the main east-west axial road and the sharp bends connecting St John's Street to St Mary's Street and Broad Street to Star Lane still indicate its extent. Excavations on the south side of High Street in 1965 revealed evidence of early tenth-century timber buildings constructed end-on to the street. The earlier settlement around St Peter's was probably taken over, but it remained distinct from the rest of the town right up to the Norman Conquest. It is now referred to as Queen Edith's Fee, after the wife of Edward the Confessor (1042-66), who controlled the Rutland estate via its centre at Hambleton eight miles to the west; the adjacent village of Edith Weston is named after her.

The effects of Danish migration into the East Midlands were profound. Places like Stamford were not just bastions for garrisons of soldiers, they were evolving communities of Danish and Saxon people sustained by agriculture and industry. The arrival of the Danes acted as an economic catalyst. York, Lincoln, Thetford, Norwich and Stamford experienced explosions of economic activity, aided by Viking supremacy on the seas; trading links were opened up with the Continent, particularly with the Baltic countries and Russia. Later Domesday evidence suggests that eastern England, under Danish dominance, was wealthier and more heavily populated than the rest of the country. At Stamford, the area between the two centres of early settlement, now Red Lion Square and Sheepmarket, developed into an important market place for the trading of produce both from the town's growing industries and crafts, including widespread iron smelting in the east, and from the agricultural land that surrounded the town.

The most important industry was ceramics. The Danes brought with them potters experienced in producing quality wheel-thrown pottery, a type unknown in England since the departure of the Romans; Wessex, for instance, continued to make coiled pottery. The pots they produced were similar to ceramics made in the Beauvais region in north-east France where the Danish armies also had connections. The availability of good local clays elevated Stamford into a major pottery centre. Production concentrated on cheap cooking pots for local use, but there was also a more prestigious range, now known as 'Stamford Ware', which was exported all over Britain and to the Continent using Viking trade routes. They were often decorated with a greenish glaze, an uncommon feature at the time. Kilns have been found around the edges of the early settlement, at the castle site in the west and at St Paul's Street in the east, and they indicate not only an extensive industry but also the sphere of Danish influence in the town.

The Danelaw, as this eastern area of England was later known, began to establish a cultural and political identity which differed greatly from that of old Anglo-Saxon Wessex. Up to 909, the Stamford area owed its main allegiance to the northern Danes at York and

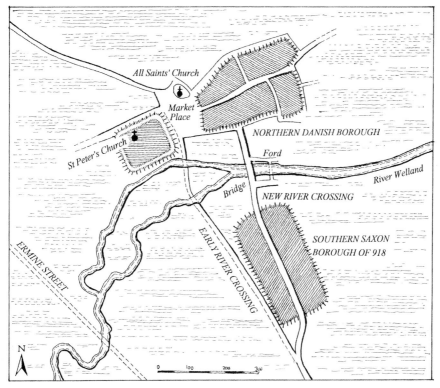

Above: *Probable development of Danish and Saxon boroughs, late 9th and early 10th centuries*

these sympathies remained in the course of later events. Many Danish place-names are found in the immediate locality: Langtoft, Wilsthorpe, Belmesthorpe, Thurlby, Carlby, Careby and Corby. The street names in Peterborough which end in *gate* (Cowgate, Westgate etc.) have Danish origins and Scotgate in Stamford is probably a Danish street name meaning a street where tolls (scutage) were collected. Finally, vestiges of the administrative organisation of land into Danish wapentakes, rather than hundreds, still survives today: Stamford is situated in the Wapentake of Ness.

Wessex responded to the Danish presence by becoming more centralised and military in character. Alfred sought co-operation with the area of Mercia that lay outside the Danelaw and his daughter Æthelflæd was married to the Mercian ruler. The reigns of Alfred's son, Edward the Elder (899-924), and his heir, Athelstan (924-39), saw the systematic reconquest of the Danelaw. The campaign was led by Edward himself and his sister Æthelflæd, 'Lady of the Mercians', who was determined to avenge the Danish raids made into Mercia in 913. In 915, Edward captured Bedford and built a second fortification, or borough, south of the Ouse to protect the river from Danish incursions. He then erected a fort at Towcester, and by 917 all the Danish armies south of the Welland had submitted to him. Æthelflæd, meanwhile, kept the Danes busy in the Midlands, gaining control of Derby and Leicester. It was at this time that the Danish borough at Stamford was probably first defended, for the *Anglo-Saxon Chronicle* records that:

> In 918 King Edward went with the army to Stamford, and ordered the borough on the south side of the river to be built; and all the people who belonged to the more northern borough submitted to him and sought to have him as their lord.

13

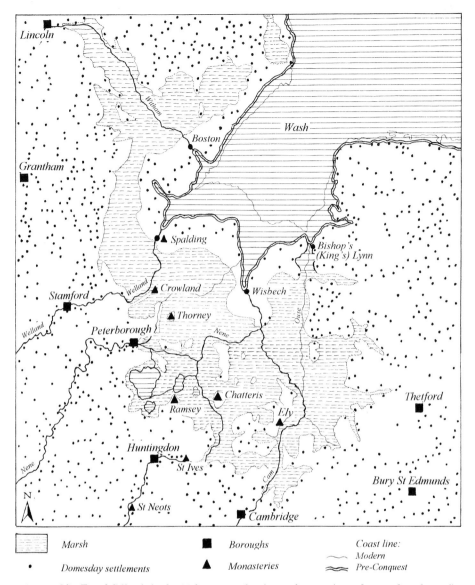

Above: *The East Midlands in the 11th century, showing settlement, rivers, fen marsh and coastline*

As at Bedford, the purpose of Edward's Stamford borough was to control the river crossing of one of the crucial waterways of eastern England; a similar bridgehead borough was built on the Trent at Nottingham. The borough was almost certainly built opposite the Danish settlement, roughly on the site of the modern St Martin's area; it would have been positioned above the flood plain with the present High Street St Martin's forming its north-south axial road and was bounded on the east by what is now Park Lane and on the south by Pinfold Lane. A bridge linking the two boroughs was probably built shortly afterwards and the contorted route taken by the new road around the northern borough is proof of that settlement's earlier existence. This new route over the river must have superseded the earlier crossing across the water meadows into the St Peter's area.

On 12 June 918, Æthelflaed died and Edward moved to the Mercian centre at Tamworth to secure the sovereignty of Wessex. Edward then pressed on north, taking

Above: Looking north from beneath the George Hotel sign; the town rises in successive tiers of stone

Nottingham, and establishing himself as the most powerful ruler in Britain; by 927 his son, Athelstan, had extended Wessex influence as far north as Penrith. But Danish allegiances remained. On Athelstan's death in 939, a Norwegian army from Ireland, led by Olaf Guthfrithson, swept through the Midlands encountering little resistance. Stamford came under his control and a base was established at Leicester. Olaf's death in 941, though, reversed these successes and allowed King Edmund (939-46), brother and successor of Athelstan, to recover the land quickly.

It is shortly after this time that we first hear of the Five Boroughs military confederacy. Stamford, Leicester, Derby, Nottingham, and Lincoln became controlling boroughs of the Danelaw. Each centre had its own court, administration and legal identity, although subordinate to the ealdorman of the Five Boroughs; Stamford and Lincoln also had a group of lawmen who were probably suitors to the court of the ealdorman or his representative. This confederacy was possibly set up after the Wessex conquest of York in 954 to instill an identity and loyalty in the settlers of the East Midlands and to sever allegiances with Danes in the unconquered areas of Northumbria.

Stamford's new status was a confirmation of its national strategic and economic importance. It had its own administrative territory which lay to the north and east (the whole of present day Kesteven and Holland). Furthermore, its status as a borough led to the foundation of an important mint whose output was only exceeded by large towns such as London, York, Winchester, and Lincoln; trade with the Viking world meant that foreign silver from overseas commerce could be turned into English coins. It may be that the mid-Lent Fair, which was later the hub of Stamford's prosperity, originated in this period.

Unfortunately, the reigns of Edgar (957-975) and Æthelred 'the Unready' (975-1016), were less favourable. Stamford failed to become a county town and its administrative lands were lost. The reasons were both political and geographical. When the focus of national politics shifted north to the Humber area, Stamford's military significance declined. Stamford was left out on a limb, hemmed in by Northampton's territory to the south and the estate of Rutland to the west. To the east were the monasteries of Peterborough (then called Medeshamstede), refounded in 966, and Thorney, refounded in 972, as well as new monasteries such as Ramsey, founded c.969. These new, richly endowed houses were quick to compete for land and the borough south of the river soon came under the control of Peterborough Abbey. The new 'shire' system of civil and military administration devised by the Wessex monarchy endorsed these changes: all Five Boroughs of the Danelaw, except Stamford, became county towns. By 1016, when Lincolnshire is first recorded, Stamford's military and administrative functions and dependent land had already passed to Lincoln. The town retained some shire-town functions and privileges throughout the Middle Ages, but the shire system has proved so efficient and enduring that Stamford now suffers from an anomalous and isolated position at the junction of four counties.

The reign of Æthelred saw the collapse of the Wessex empire. In 1002, Viking attacks into the Danelaw intensified and Æthelred, under considerable pressure, ordered that all Danes living in England should be massacred. This extraordinary command must have created chaos in areas of heavy Danish settlement such as Stamford and prompted King Swein of Denmark to attack the following year. But it took until 1013 before Swein was successful. Arriving via the Humber, he established a base at Gainsborough and marched south with his army. The Five Boroughs confederacy collapsed and the people of the East Midlands recognised Swein as their king. Their willingness to accept the Danish king confirms their sense of identity as Anglo-Scandinavians of a Northern Danelaw. By the time of Æthelred's death in 1016, Swein was accepted as the king of England and under the rule of his son Cnut (1016-35) England effectively became part of the Danish empire. At Cnut's death the Wessex dynasty could offer no viable heir (Edward the Confessor was still in his minority) so the people of the East Midlands supported the succession of Cnut's son Harold Harefoot and afterwards Hardicnut.

On the eve of an invasion from Normandy which was to suddenly change the face of Britain, Stamford was one of the largest and most prosperous towns in the country. It was heavily populated, industrialised, defended, and a centre of trade, with good inland communications and river transport to the Wash. But Stamford's failure to become a county town was a crucial factor which continues to have an adverse effect on its prospects.

Opposite: *Detail of west door at St Leonard's Priory, early 12th century*

NORMANS,
CHURCHES & TRADE

1 0 6 6 S A W A transference of power that changed the nature of English society. England was severed from its recent Scandinavian traditions to become part of a Norman world ruled by former Danes from Normandy. The reign of Edward the Confessor (1042-66) had established close ties with the duchy of Normandy and it is possible that, lacking an heir, Edward had offered the throne to Duke William. Whatever, on Edward's death, William seized his opportunity. Harold Godwineson of Wessex had already laid claim to the English throne, but having fought a Norwegian invasion force at the Battle of Stamford Bridge just east of York, his weakened army was defeated by the Normans at the Battle of Hastings. William was crowned in Westminster Abbey on Christmas Day, 1066. The threat of a new royal family, a new ruling class, and a new culture and language incited opposition from some of the eastern and northern Scandinavian settlements. Rebellion broke out in the fens aided by the arrival of the Danish fleet: Peterborough Abbey, with its new French abbot, was sacked in 1070 and the opposition held out at Ely until October 1071. Hereward the Wake, who was probably one of Edward the Confessor's thegns, is traditionally credited with leading the rising. However, there is no evidence for this, nor for his ownership of Bourne, ten miles north-east of Stamford.

For Stamford, the Norman Conquest saw the re-emergence of the town's military role. King William was anxious to impose Norman rule on the North and it was essential to secure routes of communication, particularly at towns like Stamford, which had a strong Danish identity. Stamford was one of the few 'non-county' towns in England in which the King built a castle within a year or two of the Battle of Hastings. The old enclosure next to St Peter's Church offered the best defensible position and Domesday tells us that five *mansiones* (areas of land containing a number of houses) were removed to make way for a wooden motte and bailey castle. The castle was the symbol of Norman power, reminding the townspeople of who was in control; later it became the centre of power of one of the main manors in the town. Originally it was a relatively small structure: the artificial motte or mound, on top of which was built the keep, now supports the bus station, while the bailey or service area stood to the south, towards the river. Certainly, by 1070 the town was considered safe, for the Abbot of Peterborough took refuge in Stamford with 160 knights while rebels plundered his abbey.

Having secured national stability, William was anxious to assess land ownership and wealth in his new kingdom; in 1086 he commissioned his famous Domesday Survey. This survey revealed a land deeply scarred by conquest. Many thegns or lords had lost their lands to an honorial barony who spoke French and were linked by ties of vassalage to the new sovereign. The levers of power in English society had been exploited. Many barons had married English heiresses and the borough organisation had been used to facilitate easy settlement; we know that foreign merchants and Jews were living in Stamford soon after the Conquest. There were property rewards for those loyal to the Crown: Countess Judith, William's niece, was granted considerable estates in Stamford, although she only had title to her lands through her English husband, Waltheof. Although Queen Edith, the widow of Edward the Confessor, still held the old Rutland estate of St Peter's, this was soon absorbed into the rest of the town.

Domesday provides a unique insight into the character of Stamford at the time of the Norman Conquest. As might be expected, Stamford gives the impression of being a county

Above: *Stamford Castle; base of circular 12th-century stone keep, excavated in 1933. Now destroyed* (Museum)

town, but without the status. Together with Winchcombe (Gloucs.) and Torksey (Lincs.), it was the only non-county Midlands town to be given a full survey. The town was classed as a royal borough with no overlord other than the king. There were about 412 *mansiones* in the five wards north of the river, suggesting a total population of some 2-3,000; details of the sixth ward of St Martin's were omitted as this area was administered by Northamptonshire. This means that Stamford was the second largest town in the East Midlands, after Lincoln, and one of the ten biggest urban areas in England. Leicester, Northampton and Huntingdon were all smaller and Derby and Nottingham were even less developed. Of the five churches mentioned in the survey, only two were named: St Peter's and All Saints'. All Saints' stood in the busy market area between the St Peter's settlement and the old Danish borough. The probable location of two of the other churches suggests areas of early suburban expansion. One was probably St Clement's, which stood just off the road to the north (Scotgate) and the other, Holy Trinity, stood to the east outside the later town walls. This shows that by 1086 the town had already grown to the size of the historic centre we know today; indeed the population of Stamford was no greater by the seventeenth century. Domesday also provides evidence of Stamford's industrial base, with reference to at least one mill, probably King's Mill on Bath Row. For the Normans, therefore, Stamford was a successful and prosperous market town offering the prospect of lucrative rewards.

Although national politics in the eleventh and twelfth centuries were involved almost exclusively with controversy and conflict within the Norman ruling elite, with most of the events taking place in France and the South, some had a more direct effect on Stamford. After the death of Henry I in 1135, his nephew, Stephen of Blois, seized the English throne. Henry's appointed heirs, his daughter Matilda and her husband Geoffrey Plantagenet of Anjou, retaliated by beginning a campaign to regain their inheritance. This led to their son Henry of Anjou controlling Normandy and invading England in 1153. He marched with his army through the Midlands; and while Stephen was away claiming Ipswich castle,

Above: *West front of St Leonard's Priory, early 12th century*

Stamford castle was besieged and captured. The death of Stephen's son forced a reconciliation, Stephen accepting Henry as his heir.

In 1156, Henry II (1154-89) granted the castle manor and control of the borough of Stamford to Richard du Hommet, Constable of Normandy, Sheriff of Rutland, friend and loyal supporter. His holding of the borough probably resulted in the interests of the Norman priory of St Fromond. In 1204, when King John (1199-1216) lost control of Normandy, William Hommet (Richard's son) chose to return to France. The king's cousin, William de Warenne, who had lost his French lands, was compensated with the Stamford borough and manor together with other estates around the country including Ketton, four miles to the west, and Grantham. The Warennes' main residence was at Lewes in Sussex, so, like the Hommets, he controlled the town (excluding the St Martin's area) via a steward and bailiffs. Their headquarters was the castle which was also host to the court of Stamford and the prison. The Warennes, like other lords such as the abbot of Peterborough, gained revenue from produce grown in the open fields, from rent from tenants in their manor, from local mills in their control and from tolls extracted from the markets and courts. For example, fenland cattle owners who came to sell hides to the town's thriving tanning industry had to pay tolls for the privilege. In return, the lord had to provide military service to the king as well as protection for the town. Of course it was generally in the lord's interest to work with the leading burgesses and this was particularly important in towns like Stamford which had some tradition of self-government.

When the Hommets took over the borough in the mid twelfth century they encountered a rapidly changing local economy. The pottery industry was in decline as new centres opened up, such as Bourne, ten miles to the north-east. The gap was filled by wool and grain. Norman trading routes into Flanders and the Mediterranean meant that English wool was becoming increasingly sought after abroad; demand for grain was also growing. The local limestone uplands around Stamford provided excellent grazing and arable conditions and the town found itself at the centre of one of the country's main grain- and wool-producing areas. Crowland Abbey, about twelve miles east of Stamford, which was rebuilt by Geoffrey of Orleans in the early twelfth century, amassed huge sheep herds. Stamford, aided by its experience of international trade, became a major collecting centre. Flat-bottomed boats navigated the River Welland to the Wash where goods were transferred to ships at the busy ports of Boston, Bishop's (later King's) Lynn and Spalding. The arrival of wool into the town had another benefit: it allowed a cloth industry to develop. Wool was woven into a high quality twill material called *haberget* which gained a fine reputation and was exported all over Europe where it competed favourably with Continental cloths.

Under the Normans, Stamford's mid-Lent fair became an event of international importance lasting up to three weeks. By the thirteenth century, if not before, kings were sending servants to the fair to buy cloth and luxury foreign goods for court. Merchants from Germany, France, Italy and Holland attended and some, such as Eustace Malherbe and Terricus from Cologne, bought property and settled in the town. Personal wealth is inferred from the surviving remains of some large twelfth-century stone-built houses, particularly Nos. 9-10 St Mary's Hill, where a zig-zag decorated arch now leads into a narrow passage. Stamford's borough status encouraged settlers, and a large and wealthy Jewish community developed at the western end of High Street. Jews arrived in England with the Normans and, as Christians could not engage in usury, they had an instant monopoly over the country's money-lending and banking operations. However, the Crusades, championed by Richard I (1189-99), fostered a wave of anti-semitic hysteria, fuelled by resentment of Jewish wealth and privilege. In 1189, Stamford's Jews were forced to take refuge in the castle and the following year the Jewish community at York was massacred. Further attacks occurred at Stamford in 1223 and 1242 and their synagogue was apparently burnt.

The bridging of the River Trent at Newark in the second half of the twelfth century was to have a huge impact on the prosperity of Stamford. It altered the course of the main

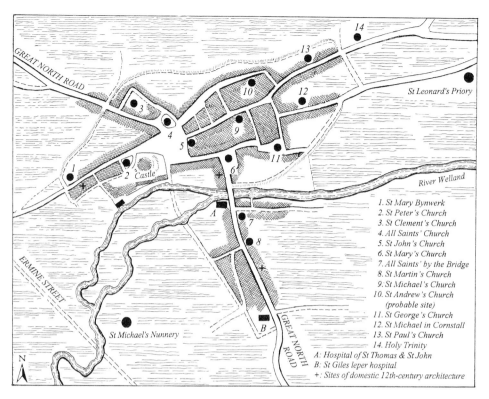

1. St Mary Bynwerk
2. St Peter's Church
3. St Clement's Church
4. All Saints' Church
5. St John's Church
6. St Mary's Church
7. All Saints' by the Bridge
8. St Martin's Church
9. St Michael's Church
10. St Andrew's Church
    (probable site)
11. St George's Church
12. St Michael in Cornstall
13. St Paul's Church
14. Holy Trinity
A: Hospital of St Thomas & St John
B: St Giles leper hospital
+: Sites of domestic 12th-century architecture

London to York road (Great North Road) so that it passed through Stamford and Grantham rather than Nottingham. More than ever, Stamford became a place for passing through, and the economic benefits must have been considerable. The town saw the comings and goings of kings and queens, barons and lords, bishops and abbots, pilgrims and preachers, merchants and salesmen, knights and soldiers, masons and artists and messengers and entertainers. There had probably been a bridge over the Welland since the early tenth century, but it was rebuilt to cater for the increased traffic. The resulting stone-built five-arched structure survived until 1845, by which time its single carriageway was an obstacle to traffic flow. A comparable but later-medieval bridge can still be seen on the River Nene at Wansford, six miles south of the town.

The Normans were not just concerned with trade; they were also interested in spiritual matters. The Conquest coincided with a spread of Church reform across the whole of Western Europe and it is in this period that most churches and monasteries in the country were founded. In 1066, there were just 50 religious houses and perhaps 1,000 monks in England; by 1216 there were around 700 houses and 13,000 monks. The great fenland abbeys of Peterborough, Crowland, Ramsey and Thorney and the new cathedral at Ely were all rebuilt using the Romanesque style of architecture, a style that had actually arrived from France before the Conquest (see St Mary's Church at Stow, north-west of Lincoln and

Above: *The Norman town*
Opposite top: *The Town Bridge was rebuilt in the 12th century,*
probably after the diversion of the Great North Road. The present bridge was built in 1849
Opposite below: *12th-century remains (buttress and parapet) at St Paul's Church, now Stamford School Chapel*

Holy Trinity at Great Paxton south of Huntingdon).

In Stamford, Durham Abbey founded St Leonard's Priory and Peterborough Abbey founded St Michael's Nunnery. St Leonard's was a Benedictine house set up in the early twelfth century to manage Durham's property in the East Midlands. Later on it prepared students for further education at Durham Hall at Oxford University. It stood to the east of the town near the River Welland and the nave of the building still survives. St Michael's Nunnery was established by William de Waterville, Abbot of Peterborough, in around 1155 to manage the abbey's property in the town. It stood to the west of the St Martin's settlement and housed about 40 nuns. Closely associated with it was the Hospital of St Thomas and St John and the leper hospital of St Giles. The hospital of St Thomas and St John stood at the south end of the newly-reconstructed town bridge. It was originally established by a guild of 'palmers' (pilgrims who had been to the Holy Land) to cater for the sick and poor as well as travellers, but by 1194 it was in the hands of Peterborough. St Giles' was founded by Peterborough probably in the reign of Stephen (1135-54) and stood isolated to the south beyond the St Martin's settlement. Two further monastic institutions were founded on the outskirts of the town. About one mile east on the River Gwash stood the Augustinian priory of Newstead, founded by the Albini family of Uffington and Belvoir (it was later owned by Belvoir Priory); it stood on the site of an older hospital. To the south-west a small convent was set up at Wothorpe which was later dissolved and absorbed into St Michael's Nunnery.

The Normans also brought about an explosion of parish church building. Before 1156 Stamford was a royal borough and the absence of any overlord other than the king gave landowners, or perhaps local groups, the opportunity to establish their own churches. Stamford, today, is still a town of churches. The quest for church building was aided by the availability of good-quality local stone. Oolitic limestone was being quarried at Barnack, four miles to the south-east, from as early as the ninth century; by the tenth century it was being exported all over the region and it was used in the rebuilding of Peterborough Abbey and Ely Cathedral. By the mid twelfth century, Stamford had at least seven major churches (St Peter's, All Saints', St George's, St John's, St Martin's, St Mary's, and St Michael's) and seven suburban or lesser churches (St Clement's, Holy Trinity, All Saints' beyond the Bridge, St Andrew's, St Mary Bynwerk, St Michael in Cornstall, and St Paul's); nine of the foundations were probably post-Conquest. However, Lincoln had upwards of 40 churches at this time. Most of Stamford's churches gradually came under monastic control and were used as a means of extracting revenue. Out of fourteen, five came under the control of St Fromond's Priory in Normandy; another five fell into the hands of Peterborough Abbey via St Michael's Nunnery; and the two churches of St Mary went to Durham Abbey through St Leonard's Priory while Holy Trinity belonged to Belvoir through Newstead Priory.

Opposite: *Tower of St Mary's Church, early 13th century*

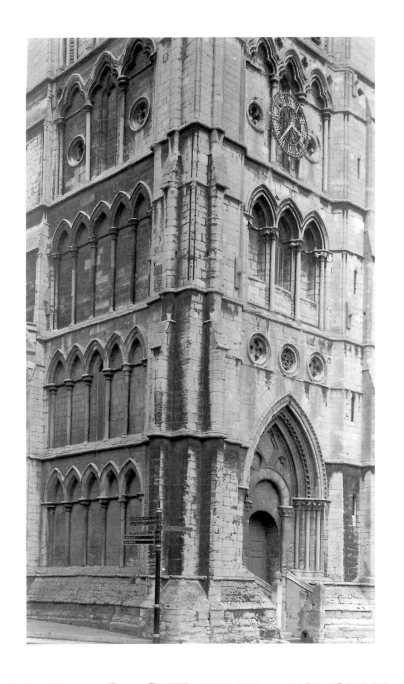

PROSPERITY
& LORDSHIP

B Y   T H E thirteenth century, Stamford was one of the largest and richest towns in England with a thriving economy based on wool and grain. However, population growth put pressure on the availability of land and jobs; lords could keep wages down and sharply rising prices forced many people into poverty and destitution.

The town also got caught up in civil war. This was fought almost exclusively between the country's powerful barons. In 1194, Richard I granted Stamford a licence to stage tournaments and these meetings gave the aristocracy the chance not only to fight but also to plot against each other. During the reigns of John (1199-1216) and his son Henry III (1216-72), Stamford was often the centre of a muster of rebellious lords and troops. In 1225, the earls of Chester, Pembroke, Gloucester, Surrey, Hereford, Derby, Warwick and others met at Stamford to question Henry III's treatment of his younger brother, Richard. Later, in 1254, civil war broke out following Henry III's embarrassing and costly campaign to defend Sicily. In the Barons' War that followed, controlling lords of Stamford were on opposing sides. The Stamford manor had reverted to the king after William de Warenne's death in 1240 and was vested in Henry's son, Edward, and his consort Eleanor. However, the Abbot of Peterborough, who controlled the St Martin's area, declared for the barons and was their treasurer in 1261. Conflict came in 1264, when the Abbot's estates in the vicinity of Stamford were plundered by the army of Henry III's brother-in-law, John de Warenne. After Henry's restoration in 1265, Warenne was rewarded with the lordship of Stamford (castle) manor and control of the borough, while the town was given grants to defend itself with more substantial town walls.

The return of the Warennes created friction in a town which, for some time, had enjoyed a fair degree of autonomy. Stamford had continued to operate as a shire-type town with burgesses and lawmen accumulating liberties and privileges; in 1202, the town had paid King John ten marks to secure full borough customs. When the borough had reverted to the king in 1240, the burgesses had re-taken control and enjoyed the associated benefits. Usually it was in the interest of the lord to work with the burgesses. However, the *Hundred Rolls*, commissioned by Edward I in 1274-5 to assess land tenure and the activities of officials, shows that the return of the Warennes brought with it a catalogue of violations against the liberty of the town. John de Warenne's stewards and bailiffs were anxious to assert and extend their privileges and corruption and extortion were common. In 1272, Thomas Savage, a prominent local figure, was arrested by Walter Dragun, Warenne's steward. He was falsely accused of harbouring thieves, was thrown into the castle prison and his house in St Martin's was plundered. Other burgesses' houses were illegally entered and robbed, while elsewhere illegal rents and tolls were seized. Grantham, which was also controlled by John de Warenne, suffered similar aggressive actions.

John de Warenne had little direct involvement with economic trade, but through his stewards he reaped the benefits of a town at its medieval economic peak. Stamford, with a population approaching 5,000, was one of the largest towns in England. It was an international trading centre for wool and grain. The *Hundred Rolls* reveal the activities of big merchant families like the Flemings and Lombards as well as lesser Florentine and French wool merchants. Stamford was also an industrial manufacturer of cloth, metal and leather,

Opposite: *Tower of St Mary's Church from south-east; early 13th century*

Above: *The Bastion on Petergate is the only surviving fragment of the late 13th-century stone town walls*
Opposite top: *All Saints' Church; the 13th-century blind arcading (beneath the aisle windows)*
was retained when the church was rebuilt in the 15th century
Opposite below: *Stamford Castle; hall service doors, late 13th century*

and the market place of the region with an extensive farming community. It had excellent limestone quarries and was probably home to a sizable community of stone-cutters and masons. The Great North Road brought English kings to the town and they sometimes held council in Stamford. But this was not always welcomed, as catering for the large royal household caused a great drain on local resources. Edward I (1272-1307) paid many visits to Stamford. His wife's funeral cortège stopped here in December 1290 and as a consequence an Eleanor Cross was later erected off Casterton Road. The town had other

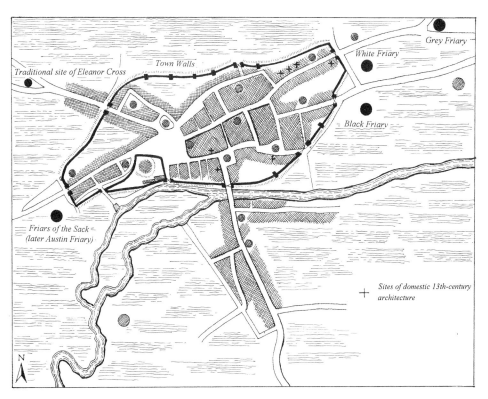

Within the map:

Grey Friary

White Friary

Town Walls

Traditional site of Eleanor Cross

Black Friary

Friars of the Sack
(later Austin Friary)

+ *Sites of domestic 13th-century*
architecture

N

attractions: the great mid-Lent fair continued to draw a whole cross-section of society and there was an annual bull-running festival, held on 13 November. The origins of bull-running in Stamford are unknown but the festival probably dated back to at least the Conquest. Bull-running also occurred at Tutbury (Staffs.), Tetbury (Gloucs.), Wisbech (Cambs.) and in the Lincolnshire village of Scrivelsby just south of Horncastle.

Prosperity, combined with new architectural developments, such as the pointed arch, presented exciting building opportunities. At No. 13 St Mary's Hill, a wealthy merchant built a large vaulted undercroft, probably twice its present size, with steps leading up to the street. Here goods were bought and sold while the merchant lived above on the ground floor. Large stone-built town houses became more common. They usually consisted of a communal hall, open to the roof, with perhaps a storeyed section at one end. The buildings on the north side of St Paul's Street still contain impressive thirteenth-century remains and many probably originated as hall houses. Although Stamford's town walls were rebuilt in wood in the 1220s, the Barons' War brought grants to renew the defences of the northern borough in stone with gates at all the entrances. The St Martin's area south of the river remained undefended as did the suburbs along Scotgate and St Paul's Street. The castle was also rebuilt and late thirteenth-century doors from the great hall still survive at the bottom of Castle Dyke.

New architectural developments were enthusiastically adopted for church building. At Peterborough Abbey a spectacular Early English west front was added to the Romanesque

Above: *Stamford in the 13th century*
Opposite top: *Many of these houses in St Paul's Street have evolved from 13th-century stone-built hall houses*
Opposite below: *13th-century undercroft at No. 13 St Mary's Hill* (Stamford Museum)

nave. The tower of St Mary's Church is Stamford's most dramatic exposition of the new style. Proudly positioned on the hill north of the Town Bridge and dominating the southern approach to the town, the huge and ornate tower is one of the country's finest examples of Early English Gothic architecture. Of equal ostentation is the magnificent south arcade of All Saints' Church. Here the arcade piers are surrounded by multiple shafts with luxuriant stiff leaf capitals derived from contemporary work at Lincoln Cathedral.

The parochial pattern of the Church was fixed well before the start of the thirteenth century and monasteries began to concentrate on ambitious programmes of land acquisition. However, this system was challenged by the arrival of the mendicant or begging orders of friars. Friaries were quite distinct from monasteries. They were international in organisation. Friars did not belong to a particular house and were free to move around, while, in accordance with the principles of St Francis and St Dominic, they were not supposed to own property and had to feed themselves by begging or doing manual labour. During the first half of the thirteenth century all four main orders of friars arrived in England and all four settled in Stamford, indicating the town's high status; important towns like Leicester, Chester and Southampton were much less favoured. A Greyfriary was established in Stamford within six years of the arrival of the Friars Minor, or Franciscans, in England. It was first recorded in 1230, and like all the new friaries was situated on the edge of the main town. It was also the largest and most magnificent of the new establishments. Built on land at the east end of St Paul's Street it housed up to 46 friars; its grand buildings, contradicting the order's austere principles, were host to passing royalty and meetings of the provincial chapter. The Black Friars (Dominicans) arrived next, building on a site just outside St George's Gate, and the White Friars (Carmelites) built their complex on land between St Paul's Street and St Leonard's Street. The last to arrive were the Friars of the Sack who chose a site outside St Peter's Gate on the opposite side of town.

Opposite: *Detail of the 14th-century broach spire of St Mary's Church*

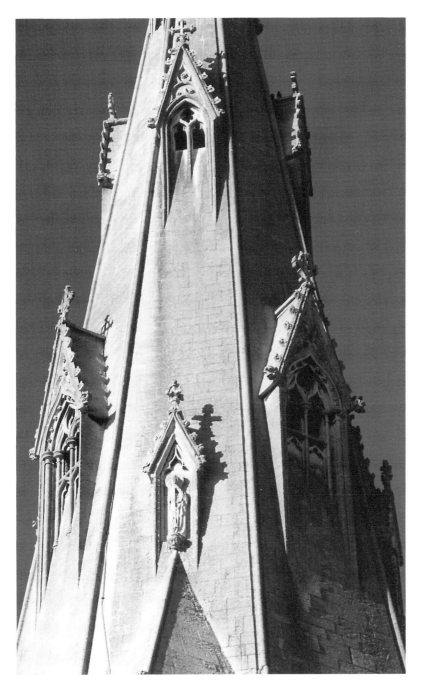

BLACK DEATH,
WAR & DECLINE

IN THE fourteenth century, the bubble of prosperity burst. Kings from Edward III (1327-77) to Henry VI (1422-61) devoted themselves to Continental campaigns, and the Hundred Years' War with France was a constant drain on the country's resources. In the long term, it also achieved very little; the great gains made in France by Edward III and Henry V (1413-22) were all lost under Henry VI. For those taking part in the fighting, war was a lucrative business for, as the feudal system declined, money was increasingly paid for recruitment. It was also a romantic enterprise; in 1348 Edward III founded the Order of the Garter as a community of knights modelled on the fellowship of King Arthur and the Round Table.

Towns like Stamford paid the price of these protracted wars. Edward I had already dealt a blow when he expelled the Jewish community in a national purge of 1290. The banking interests of Stamford's Jews had put them at the heart of the town's economy, but Edward now had new banking friends in Italy. The Hundred Years' War imposed export restrictions and taxes and prevented French merchants from attending the mid-Lent fair in large numbers. Edward III also attempted to use foreign merchants to finance the costly war. The fair, which had been at the hub of Stamford's commercial life, steadily declined throughout the fourteenth century; sales of wool dropped dramatically and Stamford's role as a collecting centre diminished. In 1353, an attempt was made to get Stamford recognised as a 'staple' town (a centre for the sale and export of wool), but this was no more than an effort to restore confidence. The amount of wool exported through the eastern ports fell consistently during the century; even Lincoln, the county town, was suffering.

The decline in wool sales was not compensated for by growth in the cloth trade. Stamford's luxury cloth industry had died out in the previous century, ruined by high costs and cheap imports from Flanders. When a new cloth industry emerged in the fourteenth century, it produced cheaper, coarser cloths using new technology such as the water-powered fulling mill and horizontal treadle loom. And it was areas like the West Midlands and the West Riding of Yorkshire, with their fast flowing streams, which became centres of this new profitable trade. East Anglia, on the other hand, rose to prominence with the arrival of skilled Flemish weavers who bypassed the monopolistic trade guilds.

The movement of trade away from Stamford and the East Midlands caused a decline in the interest of the aristocracy. The influence of the Warennes waned as they concentrated their energies on other estates in Lincolnshire, Yorkshire and East Anglia. The battle between the Warennes and the town burgesses, which had come to a head in 1288 when the town resisted an attempt to impose new tolls and rents, was finally resolved. The Warennes conceded. From 1298, the Borough was allowed to send a representative to Parliament, although the privilege was removed in 1322 and not restored until after the Wars of the Roses (1462). From 1313, John de Warenne granted the town some degree of self-government, whereby burgesses had the right to buy and sell freely and elect an alderman to govern them. Grantham, which was also owned by Warenne, experienced a similar withdrawal of interest and subsequent establishment of self government. But the benefits for both towns were lessened by economic stagnation.

The physical effects of Warenne's withdrawal soon became evident: the castle, the

---

Opposite: *View up St Mary's Hill to the steeple of St Mary's Church, 1873* (Stamford Museum)

Above: *Greyfriars' Gate at the end of St Paul's Street. It was built in the mid 14th century*

symbol of manorial power, fell into disrepair. A survey by the king's commissioners in 1340 revealed that: 'the castle is old and the walls decayed; within are an old tower, a great hall, a chamber with solar, a chapel, a turret and a house for a prison, all of no value'. The practical role of the castle had come to an end and over the ensuing centuries the buildings were plundered for stone. The last of the Warennes died in 1347, and the manor passed to William Bohun, Earl of Northampton and cousin of Edward III. On his death the manor reverted to the king and in 1363 was settled on the king's second son, Edmund Langley, Earl of Cambridge and later Duke of York. Grantham passed into the same ownership.

The death of the last of the Warennes coincided with a great catastrophe which was to reshape the structure of English life. In June 1348, the Black Death arrived in England. Overcrowding and squalor aided the spread of what was a gruesome bubonic plague carried by fleas. In 1349 the Black Death swept through Stamford, ravaging the population. Just how many people died is not recorded but the number was substantial; between July and November six out of a total of twelve clergymen died and repeated outbreaks in 1361 and 1375 further reduced the population. The plague accentuated the problems caused by economic decline. The town suburbs contracted. The church of St Michael in Cornstall had already closed in the early years of the century, its parish being absorbed into St George's. The parish of St Clement's near Scotgate was described as being 'much reduced because of the plague' and, together with Holy Trinity, it had to resort to special measures to support its clergy. Property within the walled town became derelict and many vacant plots are referred to in Stamford deeds.

This sudden reduction in local and national population, though, offered new opportunities for surviving labourers. Shortage of labour led to a rise in workers' wages. There was a decline in unfree tenures on land and lords were forced to substitute cash rents for labour services. The increased bargaining power of the workers encouraged bold action: the so-called Peasants' Revolt of 1381 was sparked off by resentment of new poll taxes and frustration with the feudal system. Riots occurred in Peterborough, and Hugh Dispenser, Bishop of Norwich, who was returning from Stamford, was forced to disperse the rebels. Living conditions might have improved as towns became less overcrowded; it would be another three centuries before national population levels returned to those of the early fourteenth century.

The deterioration of Stamford's trading prospects and the Black Death disaster might account for the lack of surviving fourteenth-century architecture in the town. No notable secular buildings and very little church building survives. The only ambitious projects were at St Mary's Church. Here, the wealthy guilds of Corpus Christi and St Mary (see below) added a north chapel; they may also have been involved in the erection of the huge broach spire onto the tower, a daring but successful feat of architectural engineering. Alterations to the nave of St George's Church, on the other hand, reveal patchy and indifferent workmanship.

The friaries, however, remained prosperous. Because friars were willing to go out into the community, giving sermons and hearing confessions, they appealed to the non-literate labouring classes. Congregations subsequently declined in the parish churches. The friaries also benefited from the patronage of rich and poor, including the king, who occasionally stopped and held court in the Stamford friaries. The Stamford Greyfriary enjoyed aristocratic support: Joan Holland (the Fair Maid of Kent), daughter of the Earl of Kent, wife of the Black Prince and mother of Richard II, was buried here in 1385 beside her first husband, Sir Thomas de Holland, in a 'sumptuous chapel' adjacent to the choir. Also buried here was Blanche, Lady Wake, daughter of Henry, Earl of Lancaster. The gatehouse onto St Paul's Street was rebuilt, bearing the arms of Edward III, and still survives in altered form. In 1341, the Austin Friars took over the site of the Friars of the Sack on the opposite side of town. They built a new church and twelve friars were initially in residence.

It is for education, however, that Stamford is mainly remembered in this period. We know that St Leonard's Priory already had a reputation for academic studies and prepared students for Durham's college at Oxford University. We know also that in 1301 Robert Luterell of Irnham gave some property in St Peter's Street to the Lincolnshire priory of

Sempringham to be used as a chantry chapel and school for novices. Here, students of the Gilbertine order studied divinity and philosophy in much the same way as students at Oxford and Cambridge. The friaries certainly encouraged education; they were keen to promote learning and were particularly influential at Oxford University. The Franciscan Greyfriary at Stamford educated its novices, but there is no evidence to suggest that any of the friaries had colleges in the town itself.

In 1333, though, an event occurred which was to capture the imagination of generations of later historians. At the time, Oxford was plagued by violent disputes. The university and the town were at war and within the university northern masters and students were fighting against what they saw as the dominance of southern interests. The result was that a frustrated northern faction left. They went firstly to Northampton where an earlier splinter university had been briefly set up in 1264. The town proved unsuitable and so they moved on to Stamford. Here they found a peaceful site, conducive to, and with some tradition of, academic study. But their stay was short lived. Both Oxford and Cambridge Universities, fearing the potential rivalry of a third university, petitioned the king, the queen and the Bishop of Lincoln to outlaw the Stamford assembly. The power of the established universities was too strong: just as Oxford had crushed the splinter university at Northampton in 1264, so it took less than two years for the last of the students and masters to be rooted out of Stamford and sent back to Oxford.

The event was to have repercussions for centuries afterwards. Oxford, anxious to avoid a repeat exodus, made its students swear: 'that you will not lecture or attend lectures at Stamford, as in a university or general school or college'. John Hardyng, a fifteenth-century poet and chronicler, invented a story of how King Bladud, the father of King Lear, had founded a great university at Stamford in 872BC. Later in the eighteenth century, the antiquarian William Stukeley 'discovered' the remains of many academic halls which he claimed had been owned by the great monastic houses of England. As the town became more provincial, so a mythical 'golden age' became more attractive. Finally, in 1890 Brasenose College, Oxford, removed the ancient 'Brazenose' knocker from a thirteenth-century doorway in St Paul's Street and carried it in triumph to Oxford. They believed that the knocker had originally been brought from Oxford in 1333 and that this was the site of the secession. However, there is no evidence to support any of this.

Opposite: West end of All Saints' Church rebuilt by the Browne family in the late 15th century

PRIVATE WEALTH,
PUBLIC SQUALOR

THE RESOLUTION of the Hundred Years' War in the mid fifteenth century did nothing to help Stamford's bleak economic situation. The Lancastrians, who had seized the throne in 1399, made great gains in France under Henry V, but then lost everything in 1453 under Henry VI. England even lost the south-western territory of Gascony which had been the source of a lucrative wine and cloth trade since the twelfth century. What followed was one of the most turbulent decades in English history, known popularly as the Wars of the Roses. Henry VI suffered a mental breakdown and the absence of a strong king stirred up unrest among the county's leading magnates. Leadership of the country was contested between Richard, Duke of York, who was supported by the Nevilles (Earls of Salisbury) and the Earl of Warwick, and John Beaufort, Duke of Somerset, who was supported by Queen Margaret and the court. During the winter of 1451-52, York and his agents stirred up unrest in the West Country and the East Midlands. The manor of Stamford had been owned by the York family since 1363 and the town was the centre of a rising involving reinforcements from other local Yorkist estates like Grantham and Fotheringhay. Although York and the Nevilles gained the upper hand after the death of Somerset at the Battle of St Albans in 1455, Queen Margaret gradually strengthened her hold on the country's administration so that by 1459 she was determined to crush her enemies.

Initial battles in 1459 forced York to flee the country, but on his return in October the following year, he claimed the throne. However, York was defeated and killed at the Battle of Wakefield. A triumphant Queen Margaret marched south to meet the Earl of Warwick at St Albans, sacking centres of Yorkist sympathy on the way. Stamford was plundered during February 1461: some of the town's ancient records were burned and damage was probably inflicted on property. However, the survival of new stained glass in the windows of St John's and St George's Churches suggests that destruction was minimal.

Margaret defeated Warwick at St Albans but she failed to secure London, which refused to open its gates. Meanwhile, Edward, Richard of York's son, had defeated a Lancastrian force in the West and he marched to London where, with the help of Warwick, he was welcomed and proclaimed king. His claim was consolidated by victory in another bitter battle at Towton in Yorkshire.

Loyal Stamford was rewarded early in the following year with a charter of incorporation. A borough council was set up, under an alderman or mayor, based on the established system of an upper and lower council each of twelve members, both elected by freemen of the town. There was to be a town bench of Justices of the Peace and the new Corporation was to be represented in Parliament by two MPs. The royal arms were combined with those of the Warenne family to create a Borough shield. Grantham received a similar charter the following year.

But Edward IV's marriage into the Woodville family and their sudden rise to political prominence created resentment among many of the country's great magnates. Furthermore, Edward's foreign policy alienated his brother, the Duke of Clarence, and Edward's 'kingmaker' the Earl of Warwick. They encouraged rebellion, and in 1470 Sir Robert Welles, son of Lord Willoughby de Eresby, was persuaded to lead a Lincolnshire rising against the king. Edward and his army travelled to Stamford to meet the rebels and the two sides met at a site just off the Great North Road, five miles north-west of the town.

Opposite: *All Saints' Church from Red Lion Square*

Above: *St John's Church, rebuilt by a wealthy syndicate in the 1450s*

Edward had Welles' father in custody and beheaded him before the battle. Unnerved, Welles' army fled when the king's artillery fired, throwing off their coats to aid their retreat; the meeting was later named the Battle of Losecoat Field. Robert Welles was captured and promptly executed and the village of Pickworth was destroyed; Warwick and Clarence fled to France. As a last resort, Warwick and Clarence formed an alliance with the exiled Lancastrian queen and, in July 1470, Henry VI was restored to the throne. Edward escaped to Burgundy, but support for Henry was fragile and prompted Edward's return the following year. He arrived with an army which defeated and killed Warwick, extinguished the Lancastrian royal line and suppressed the Yorkist dissidents.

Once secure, Edward IV set out on a period of constructive rule based on shrewd fiscal policy. In 1481, Edward awarded Stamford a second charter which concentrated on economic issues. A new weekly market was created and two new fairs were sanctioned. The Corporation was given property so that it could maintain the town walls, but it is clear that

Above: *St Martin's Church, rebuilt in the 1480s by the Bishop of Lincoln*

the new independent town was looking to desperate measures to improve its economic situation.

The reality was that all the wealth lay in the hands of a few individuals while the majority suffered as industry and markets declined. The decline in wool sales and the migration of the cloth industry created a recession in which the remaining trade was concentrated in the hands of those few individuals who were big enough to weather it. The 1379 poll-tax returns for Stamford reveal a social distinction that was to dominate town life in the fifteenth century. They show the dominance of an elite group of rich wool merchants, people like Geoffrey Casterton, John Browne, William de Styandebey and John Spicer, the wealthiest of whom paid the same tax as all the bakers, brewers and innkeepers put together. Others fell by the wayside. Thomas Kesteven was a local wool merchant who, like the big wool traders, was a member of the English-owned wool staple at Calais in France; the Calais staple was a vital link for trade with the Continent. He stumbled on hard times

Above: *East end of St Martin's Church*
Opposite: *Browne's Hospital, Broad Street, is an important medieval almshouse dating from the 1470s*

and in 1482 lamented: 'I see daily kings, princes and other estates from the highest to the lowest brought down, now high, now low, now rich, now poor, now alive, now dead. He that has his life and has nothing, that previously had riches, is worst at ease.' As the focus of national trade shifted from the eastern ports to London so this trend was intensified; most occupations began to rely on local rather than national and overseas commerce.

The most prominent family in the town were the Brownes, whose lavish brasses still decorate the floor of All Saints' Church. The Brownes were wool merchants and members of the wool staple at Calais; it is possible that the large timber-framed building overlooking Red Lion Square (Nos. 6-7) was the Brownes' woolhouse. Their wealth and domination of the town was confirmed in stone when they rebuilt most of All Saints' Church in the 1470s and 80s. The tower with its soaring pinnacle spire was an elegant match for the old steeple of St Mary's.

William Browne was the most outstanding member of the family; Leland, writing in the mid-sixteenth century, described him as 'a merchant of very wonderfulle richnesse'. But he was without a male heir. So, for posterity, he established an almshouse on Broad Street in the mid 1470s as an act of piety and as a token of his concern for the poverty in the town. This elaborate stone building with its sumptuous stained glass, chapel, cloister, and courtyard catered for no more than 12 people. He failed to establish the charity officially and it was his brother-in-law, Thomas Stokes, Canon of York, who formally set it up in 1489, after Browne's death. William's death meant that the family business went into the hands of his nephew, Christopher, but Stamford's increasing provincialism soon forced the operation to move to London.

The Brownes exemplified a new mood of personal piety which was to have a great effect upon the town. The focus of this piety was not the monasteries and friaries, but the parish church and the town itself. The friaries and monasteries had fallen out of favour. Chaucer's *Canterbury Tales* had revealed the extent of corruption among friars as early as the mid fourteenth century. Scandals were common and St Michael's Nunnery was notorious for its intrigues and mismanagement. Fewer and fewer friars, monks and nuns lived in the great religious houses that surrounded the town and by the sixteenth century St Leonard's Priory was occupied only by a caretaker. The parish church became the new focus of patronage and as the monasteries declined, many of the churches were taken over by secular groups. In the early fifteenth century, the churches of St George's, St John's, St Peter's and St Paul's passed into the hands of a wealthy local syndicate who controlled them until the Reformation.

Trade guilds became important benefactors. Guilds were monopolistic organisations designed to protect particular trades and crafts. They dictated trading practices for each industry and ensured that economic control of the town remained in the hands of the burgesses. The guilds were also concerned with piety and indulged in opening chapels and repairing churches. The Corpus Christi Guild was probably Stamford's richest. It is first heard of in the mid-fourteenth century, when, together with the Guild of St Mary, it built the north chapel of St Mary's Church. By the beginning of the fifteenth century, the Corpus Christi had accumulated property all over the town and its guildhall stood on the site of No. 4 St Mary's Place where a late fourteenth-century undercroft still survives. Most of the parish churches had their guilds, such as St Martin's, which provided a bull for the annual bull-running on 13 November, and many must have contributed to general rebuilding work.

All of Stamford's surviving medieval churches were rebuilt in the mid to late fifteenth century. Many of the churches must have been in a poor state of repair and this was probably a major factor in the decision to rebuild; only the best of the early work was retained. The wealthiest church at the time was St John's which was completely rebuilt by a number of rich patrons around 1451 and equipped with a superb angel roof, elaborate screens and stained glass. The Browne family responded with the even more flamboyant rebuilding of All Saints' Church. Sir William Bruges, Garter King of Arms, provided money in his will for rebuilding the chancel of St George's Church, together with a series of stained glass windows depicting the Knights of the Garter. William Hykeham, a local baker and alderman, remodelled the Corpus Christi Chapel in St Mary's Church, furnishing it with a magnificent ceiling adorned with golden bosses; the splendid tomb of Sir David Phillip was built next to the altar in 1506. St Michael's Church on High Street received extensive alterations; St Mary's Church got a new nave, while St Martin's Church was totally rebuilt on a grand scale in the 1480s, under the auspices of John Russell, the bishop of Lincoln. An attempt was even made to establish a new civic festival to celebrate the churches' patronal grants.

The grand rebuilding of Stamford's main churches hastened the decline of the town's suburban foundations. Stamford no longer had the population or resources to maintain all its churches. All Saints' beyond the Bridge had been annexed to St Martin's as early as 1434; the private chantry in St Clement's became more important than the church itself, while the parish of Holy Trinity, containing only ten residents, was forced to form a guild to support its rector whereby the church was renamed St Stephen. St Mary Bynwerk on the opposite side of the town was another poor foundation, and although it was not amalgamated with St Peter's until 1462, it had probably ceased to function earlier in the century. St Paul's was also experiencing difficulties: by 1466 its parish had been grouped with Holy Trinity, while its private guild of St Katherine, refounded in 1480 by William Browne, was more wealthy than the church.

Opposite: Courtyard elevation of Burghley House, built by William Cecil between 1555 and 1587

MONASTERIES
TO MANORS

EDWARD IV'S premature death in 1483 gave Richard of Gloucester the chance to usurp the throne. But Richard III, who was born at the Yorkist castle of Fotheringhay, just south of Stamford, encountered general hostility, particularly after suspicion arose over the death of Edward IV's two sons. Opposition was led by Henry Tudor, Earl of Richmond; his mother, Lady Margaret Beaufort, and the Duke of Buckingham. Events finally led to the Battle of Bosworth Field in August 1485 where Richard III was slain.

Henry VII (1485-1509) tentatively brought in the Tudor dynasty. Its succession was never particularly secure and this insecurity is crucial in understanding Henry VIII's divorces and obsession for a male heir. Henry VII quickly capitalised on the centralisation policies of Edward IV and Richard III and the rise of the nation state became a crucial part of Tudor policy. Power was increasingly concentrated in the south-east within the two leading cities of London and Norwich; by the seventeenth century London was twenty times the size of the next largest city. This move towards centralised government was part of a pan-European movement which included new religious and secular ideas. These ideas could now be broadcast using Gutenberg's invention of the printing press. In Germany, Luther's programme for a reformed church, produced in response to a corrupt Catholic Church, formed the basis of the Protestant movement. In Italy and other countries new ideas of Renaissance humanism were spreading.

Henry VIII (1509-47), however, was the catalyst who brought these issues to a head. In his need for a male heir, Henry forced through a series of acts which made him supreme head of a Church of England divorced from Rome. The friaries and monasteries, with their papal connections, were now seen as a potential threat. Their dissolution offered many advantages. It would provide vital income for a bankrupt king, as church property and lands, which had been accumulating over the centuries, would all come to the Crown. Furthermore, the influence of rebellious factions in the northern abbeys would be reduced with the removal of abbots from the House of Lords. With the help of Thomas Cromwell, the lesser monasteries were closed down in 1536, the larger ones in 1538 and, under the direction of the Duke of Somerset in the protectorate of Edward VI, the trade guilds and private chantries were outlawed in 1547. It has been described as the greatest ever act of nationalization without compensation.

The Reformation created major changes in the Stamford area, as it did throughout the country. St Leonard's Priory, St Michael's Nunnery and Newstead Priory were all dissolved in 1536, together with the four friaries. The Gilbertine priory at Sempringham disappeared and the large fenland monasteries at Crowland, Thorney and Ramsey were shut. The monastic buildings and lands of Peterborough Abbey became the basis of one of the country's six new cathedral dioceses. The physical effect of these closures was considerable; throughout the country, great Gothic churches and monastic buildings were reduced to quarries. The disaffected, hardened by heavy taxes, organised rebellions. In October 1536, opposition broke out in north-east Lincolnshire with a call to return to the old faith. This revolt, known as the Pilgrimage of Grace, was the first of its kind in England. The Duke of Suffolk was dispatched to meet the rebels, who eventually surrendered at Stamford on 13 October just as Yorkshire was about to rise. Henry VIII, disturbed by the potential of such rebellions, condemned Lincolnshire as 'one of the most brute and beastly of the whole realm'.

What the Reformation did in Stamford, however, was to tidy up the problem of Stamford's poorer churches by providing an opportunity to re-organise parish structure. St Peter's was shut and its parish amalgamated with All Saints'; St Andrew's and St Stephen's were absorbed into St Michael's parish; St Clement's went to St John's and St Paul's parish was taken over by St George's. By 1532, St Paul's Church was being used as a free grammar school founded by merchant and alderman William Radcliffe.

Under the protectorate of Edward VI (1547-1553), Reformation ideas gained strength. Parish churches were stripped and the booty was seized by the state. The new Book of Common Prayer was in English and the second, 1552, edition was unambiguously Protestant. It formed the basis of Elizabeth I's religious settlement of 1558-9. This was engineered by William Cecil (see below), who pushed the Acts of Supremacy and Uniformity through Parliament without a single churchman's consent, thereby making constitutional history; his Catholic opponents accused him of coercion 'partly by violence and partly by fear'. The acts placated the reformists and the new challenge of Anglicanism pushed Catholicism into minority status. Miraculously, this transition was achieved without the level of strife experienced in other European countries.

Whether the people of Stamford were sympathetic to the events of the Reformation is unclear; the town's role in the Lincolnshire Rising of 1536 had been no more than marginal. On the other hand, a Dominican friar was attacked in St Martin's Church for supporting the old system and, in 1550, Hugh Latimer preached there in favour of the new changes. But St Martin's was now controlled by the Protestant Cecil family and was probably unrepresentative. It was William Cecil who helped introduce Puritan refugee weavers into Stamford in the late 1560s.

The assets of the Dissolution did not stay in the Crown coffers for long. Old monastic lands were sold off cheaply by a Tudor administration desperate for ready cash to finance its costly wars with France and Spain. During the sixteenth and early seventeenth centuries Stamford became surrounded by new and refurbished estates, many of which were established by aspiring merchants and *nouveaux riches*. The Browne family of merchants bought the medieval manor house at Tolethorpe, two miles to the north, and it was here that Robert Browne, founder of the Puritan Brownist movement, was born in *c*.1550. William Trollope of Thurlby erected a new house at Casewick, three miles to the east, while Robert Manners, who was personal attendant to Elizabeth I, had a large estate at nearby Uffington. The Noels inherited an estate at Exton, six miles to the north-west, from Sir Baptist Hicks, a rich London mercer and money lender; the Digbys of Stoke Dry had a house at North Luffenham, and Lord Willoughby de Eresby was at Grimsthorpe Castle, ten miles to the north. The area was already home to royalty: Henry VII's mother, Lady Margaret Beaufort, had a large house at Collyweston, four miles south-west of the town she now owned. The political influence of many of these families was to affect Stamford for over 300 years.

Most of the monastic land around Stamford, however, fell into the hands of the Cecil family who arrived in the area from Herefordshire. Although the Cecils were merchants and lawyers, their success largely depended on Crown offices and favours. The flux in society caused by the Reformation and the way the country was governed gave aspiring middle class families first a taste, then an appetite, for power. Minor families were suddenly able to

rise to the highest office. David Cecil was steward to Lady Margaret Beaufort and he served Henry VIII at court; from 1504 he was repeatedly elected MP and alderman (mayor) of Stamford. His son, Richard, became sheriff of Rutland and it was he who bought up most of the old monastic land. He was also the father of the family's most illustrious member, William Cecil.

William was born in 1520. He was educated at Grantham and Stamford grammar schools, St John's College, Cambridge, and later at Gray's Inn, London, where he won the favour and patronage of the Duke of Somerset; he served as Secretary to Somerset during the protectorate of Edward VI. On Elizabeth's accession in 1558, William Cecil was appointed principal Secretary of State and he was largely responsible for the tone of compromise in Elizabeth's religious settlement; a compromise, however, which was violently opposed by Cecil's cousin, Robert Browne of Tolethorpe. Cecil also succeeded in dispersing the Catholic threat, first by imprisoning their figurehead, Mary Stuart, Queen of Scotland, and then by crushing the Northern Rebellion in 1572. For his efforts, which led finally to the execution of Mary Stuart in 1587 at Fotheringhay Castle, ten miles south of Stamford, Cecil demanded a peerage. He was promptly made Lord Burghley, taking his title from the huge house he was building just outside his home town.

But Cecil and Elizabeth were unable to control the new forces in society. The feudal notion of the king or queen as the principal landowner and source of ultimate justice was now a thing of the past. The monopoly of the Church over cultural and intellectual life was shattered. In addition there was the growth of a new middle class eager for power. Ultimately Elizabeth left the English state ungovernable, riddled with inefficiency, debt and corruption. Cecil himself diverted state money into his own pocket. From 1572 until his death in 1598, Cecil was Lord Treasurer; in Parliament, he complained of tax cheating, assessing his own salary at just £133 per year. His real income, of which two thirds was creamed off from the profits of his office, was nearer £4,000 per year, yet he still succeeded in evading tax! Between 1608 and 1612, Robert Cecil, his son, received £6,900 per year from political offices at a time when the national debt was in the region of £400,000.

For over thirty years William Cecil devoted a good proportion of his money to building two palatial 'prodigy' mansions, one for himself at Theobalds, near Cheshunt (Herts.; now demolished) and one for his mother in the manor of Little Burghley just outside Stamford. Burghley House was completed in 1587 and was one of the largest and most opulent of the great Elizabethan mansions, happily mixing fashionable Renaissance details with familiar medieval forms such as the turreted gatetower. The house was surrounded by a great park which was extended in 1576-8 when Cecil obtained land that had belonged to Peterborough Abbey.

Although Cecil rarely visited Burghley, he quickly set about asserting his authority over Stamford. During the 1550s he secured the manor of St Cuthbert's Fee which had formerly belonged to Durham Abbey. In 1560, he persuaded Elizabeth to grant him the lordship of St Martin's and when, in the following year, the town asked Cecil to ensure for them control of the Stamford (castle) manor from the Crown, Cecil had the audacity to take it for himself.

Cecil was now lord of all Stamford and, for the first time since the Warennes, the town

Opposite top: *The grand west front of Burghley House*
Opposite middle: *Tolethorpe Hall, 2 miles north of Stamford, rebuilt by the Browne family*
Opposite below: *Casewick Hall, 3 miles east of Stamford, rebuilt in the early 17th century*

experienced the effects of an interfering landlord. Of course, Stamford was not unusual in this respect; most sixteenth-century English towns were run by wealthy families as oligarchies. Cecil became Recorder of the town, that is the highest justice in the area. Like his predecessors, he nominated the town's MPs: between 1504 and 1589 five members of the Cecil family represented Stamford in Parliament, while other MPs were selected from friends and relations. He appointed town officials and determined the election of aldermen (mayors), whose sycophantic replies to Cecil's off-hand and condescending letters reveal the new seat of power in local politics. Cecil also came to appoint the master of the grammar school he had attended; he even nominated the masters of Oakham and Uppingham schools, which were founded in 1584 by one of his patronees, Robert Johnson of Stamford. Finally, in 1593, Cecil got his privileges confirmed in Stamford's constitution, and bye-laws were introduced which facilitated Cecil control. In return for all this the Cecils offered the town small gifts. It was with Cecil help that in 1558 alderman John Houghton was able to build a Town Hall and Gaol at the north end of the Town Bridge and in 1570, the bridge itself was partially repaired by Cecil, as he collected the tolls from it. In 1609, Thomas Cecil gave land in the Market Deeping area to the Corporation so that revenue from the land could be used to apprentice youths in Stamford.

William Cecil died in 1598 and his canopied Renaissance tomb dominates the chancel of St Martin's Church. He left two sons by two different marriages. Robert Cecil took over his father's professional responsibilities and swapped the house at Theobalds for Hatfield House (Herts.) where his descendants made their home, while Burghley was inherited by Thomas, the elder son, who had military rather than administrative interests. As Burghley had been the home of his mother, Thomas' occupation meant that a second house was required for widows of the family. For this purpose, Thomas built a large house at Wothorpe, one mile south-west of Stamford.

In 1605, James I rewarded the Cecils for their loyalty to the Crown: Thomas was created first Earl of Exeter, and his brother became Earl of Salisbury. The titles did not come with any land or rights in those areas. Cecil supremacy in the Stamford area continued under the Earls of Exeter. James I gave Thomas Cecil almost 5,000 acres of land in the immediate vicinity of Stamford, increasing the local Burghley estate to some 28,000 acres. However, the Cecil position was compromised by the situation of William, second Earl of Exeter. Lacking a male heir, he was forced to settle the manor of Stamford on his youngest daughter whereby it passed by marriage to Henry Grey of Groby (Derbs.) who became Earl of Stamford in 1628. The manor of Stamford remained out of Cecil control until 1747 when the eighth Earl bought it back.

Within fifty years the Cecils had established a framework of control which was to prevail in local politics for at least three centuries. By the early nineteenth century, Stamford was recognised as a 'pocket borough', a town fossilised and stagnated by Cecil ascendancy and its associated corruption. In Drakard's *History of Stamford*, published in 1822, William Cecil is seen as the man who 'laid the cornerstone of corruption which has paralysed the vital energies of the town of Stamford, and of that tyranny by which the rights of the inhabitants have been held in subjection to the domination of his family'.

Opposite: *Timber-framed buildings off St Mary's Street*

RECESSION

IN 1597, William Cecil was near the end of his life and like William Browne before him, he was anxious to be remembered as a great benefactor of the town. Accordingly, he founded an almshouse. The buildings of the old monastic hospital of St Thomas and St John were converted to give accommodation for twelve poor men; proper almshouse buildings were later erected by his descendants. Almshouses are often founded in periods of economic decline and Lord Burghley's Hospital was no exception. There was no recovery of industry in sixteenth-century Stamford. As wool markets declined still further, hampered by the loss of Calais and the Staple in 1557, so leather-working of hides from fenland cattle and the weaving of fibres such as hemp became the largest industries. William Cecil attempted to build a huge hemp-beating mill, but the town was still independent enough to reject his monopolistic scheme. Cecil also supported the immigration of persecuted Puritan textile workers from Flanders. Some of these settled in Stamford in the 1560s, but in spite of financial incentives from Cecil they failed to establish a profitable industry. Lady Cecil's efforts to set up a spinning school and silk industry equally came to nothing.

What compounded the problem was that Stamford's role as an important market centre was diminishing as competition from other towns increased. For Thomas and John Hatcher, gentlemen farmers of Careby, seven miles north of the town, early seventeenth-century Stamford was just one of many markets they visited; much of the local produce went straight to the London markets. Traffic on the Great North Road was not yet heavy enough to compensate, but there were a number of large inns which catered for travellers. These included the Cecil-owned George in St Martin's; the Old Swan, the Angel of the Hoope and Black Bull in St Mary's Street, and the Blue Bell in Ironmonger Street. Changes in local agriculture also affected the town. Barley for malting now became the principal crop and the limestone heathlands were ploughed as sheep grazing moved into newly-drained areas of the fens. But Stamford was unable to capitalise on the barley. The silting up of the River Welland impeded river transport and with it the development of a malting industry. Following the flood of 1570, the town secured an Act of Parliament to make the river navigable but practical difficulties and lack of funds meant nothing was done. Until river navigation was resumed the town's prospects would continue to be stifled.

In 1541, Stamford and neighbouring Grantham were described as 'decay'd' towns of the realm. Lincoln, which was also cut off from river transport, saw its population drop from a peak of about 8,000 in the early fourteenth century to just 2,000 or so, making it no bigger than Stamford. Stamford's population remained static during a period of rapid national growth; recession probably encouraged late marriages and birth control. But rising population elsewhere created a shortage of land and food which forced up prices. Food prices in the period 1500-1640 rose eightfold while wages only increased threefold. Starvation must have been a real threat for wage-labouring families, whose living standards plummeted during these years; in the 1570s a poor-house was set up in Stamford. Many people were forced onto the roads in search of employment and Stamford, being on the Great North Road, was burdened by an influx of vagrants. In 1547, the Corporation issued an ordinance that no one should give jobs to strangers while there were native people out of work.

Opposite top: *No. 6 St Peter's Hill & No. 1 St Peter's Street. Two 16th/17th century timber-framed houses. No. 1 was remodelled in the 18th century, but the overhanging jetty is still clearly visible*
Opposite below: *Lord Burghley's Hospital, Station Road. This range was built c. 1616, altered 1964.*

Elizabeth's wars with Spain worsened the economic situation by imposing heavy demands on towns. While William Cecil evaded tax, Stamford was forced to muster troops, keep weapons and pay taxes. In 1584, the Corporation had to lease out the common tenter meadows, where cloth was hung to dry, to meet its tax responsibilities. In 1602, the town was virtually bankrupt and had to ask to be excused from paying tax. A pageant of loyalty to James I, which welcomed him when he passed through Stamford the same year, resulted in a charter which went some way towards relieving the charge.

The physical effects of economic decline were alarming. Since the fourteenth century whole areas of the town had become derelict and plots of land within the decaying town

Opposite top: *No. 19 St Mary's Street (St Mary's Vaults).*
This large timber-framed building probably originated as a 16th-century inn
Opposite below: *No. 16 Barn Hill, built as All Saints' Vicarage in the late 15th century*
Above: *No. 40 St Mary's Street; a large 16th-century timber-framed building*
Below: *King's Mill, Bath Row, rebuilt by the Cecil family around 1640*

walls stood empty. At Lincoln the contraction of the city was even more pronounced: of the 47 churches in use in the twelfth century only 14 still survived. The general poverty in Stamford was perhaps reflected by the increasing use of timber for larger buildings. Timber-framing had been used for poorer-quality housing throughout the Middle Ages, but with money in short supply it became necessary to use it on a wider scale. No. 19 St Mary's Street (St Mary's Vaults) was probably built in the late fifteenth, or early sixteenth century, as an inn for travellers. It has a timber-framed upper storey and cross wing while No. 40 St Mary's Street has a jettied upper storey with close-studded timbers. Stone was only used when patronage was forthcoming, as in the Town Hall (demolished, 1776) and in All Saints' Vicarage on Barn Hill.

Stamford, like many other English towns, had a population weakened by recession, poverty and social disorder; malnutrition and insanitary living conditions were commonplace. Plagues frequented the country and they visited the town in 1574 and 1581-2. But these were nothing compared with the epidemic of 1604 which wiped out about one third of the town's population. The Corporation made efforts to contain its contamination: visitors were banned and an isolation ward was erected, but in that year 600 people were buried rather than the usual 30 to 40. Half of Stamford's 12 clergymen died in the outbreak. The levelling effects of the plague alarmed some of the more wealthy residents who were prompted into action. Richard Snowden, vicar of St John's, died of the plague, but by his will an almshouse was founded in Scotgate for seven poor widows. A family of shoemakers called Wells, who all died of the plague, left property to set up a school, while Lady Dorothy Cecil established a further school in St Martin's. The Corporation introduced new building regulations designed to reduce multi-tenancies and increase rateable income (although they appear not to have been enforced) and the town's water system was renewed.

Economic improvement remained elusive as the town struggled in the aftermath of plague. Richard Norris began a bell-founding business in 1603 which was to become one of the most important in the East Midlands but his success was exceptional. Financial difficulties and a series of failed negotiations during the 1640s with David Cecil, the third Earl of Exeter, meant that no real progress was made on developing the river. Furthermore, between them, the Cecils and the Greys created a grain-milling and brewing monopoly which impeded progress. In the 1630s the Cecils claimed sole rights in milling and, in a violation of common rights, they cut a mill race through common land on the water meadows to power their newly rebuilt King's Mill on Bath Row. In 1641, they demanded tolls from freemen's market stalls. The Greys, as Earls of Stamford, fought for a royal grant which gave them and the Cecils exclusive control of brewing. Traders in the town were outraged and the Corporation took the case to the Privy Council which, as it consisted mainly of gentry, took the side of the Greys. Those burgesses who had dared to go against the will of Stamford's lords were humiliated and removed from office. Richard Butcher, author of the first history of Stamford published in 1646, suffered this fate and claimed that Stamford's lords were 'the towne's common enemy' who 'tossed the best of the burgesses out of their gownes'.

Opposite: Wothorpe House, built by Thomas Cecil in the early 17th century.
The house was garrisoned by the Royalists in July 1643

CIVIL WAR

T H E   F I N A L   barrier to a change in Stamford's fortunes was imposed by national events that affected every town in the land. The Civil War, which began in 1642, was brought on by many long-term underlying factors as well as the more immediate short-term events. Britain's population doubled in the period 1500-1650. The result was food shortages which led to hunger, inflation and higher taxes, and work shortages which led to unemployment and the migration of labour. In short it was a period of great upheaval and distress. This period also saw the rise of a new middle class who were eager to expand their position and role in society. Religion was of vital importance. England had become a Protestant nation where Catholicism was viewed with grave suspicion, even as treason, an attitude fuelled by the horrors of the Thirty Years' War on the Continent. James I (1603-1625) was able to weather these growing problems, despite an ineffective foreign policy and scandalous court affairs. But, like Elizabeth I, he failed to solve any of them. Instead he handed them on to Charles I, who succeeded in 1625. Unfortunately Charles was the wrong person to deal with these complex issues.

First of all he married a French Catholic princess. He then embarked on an expensive and disastrous foreign policy which was supported by tax increases, unauthorised by Parliament, which were enforced by the threat of imprisonment without trial. Objections raised in March 1629 resulted in Charles dissolving Parliament; he continued to rule without consultation for eleven years based on his belief in the Divine Right of Kings. The extension of Ship Tax to the whole of the country created great resentment as did his association with Archbishop William Laud. Laud was a high churchman who wanted to restore the authority of bishops and to regain Church lands. In a period of Puritanism, his policies were widely viewed as having an affinity with the Roman Catholic Church; they were seen as letting Popery in through the back door. Some Puritan groups had already emigrated to America (some of the first, known as the Pilgrim Fathers, were caught in 1607 at Boston, 40 miles north-east of Stamford, trying to set sail for the Continent), but the main exodus came in the 1630s when John Cotton left with a large contingent from Boston.

Disaster struck in 1637 when Charles attempted to impose Laudian-style religious reforms on the Presbyterian Church of Scotland. The result was full-scale rebellion. In the autumn of 1640, the Scots invaded England and occupied Newcastle where they remained until a treaty could be agreed. Charles, lacking the resources to muster a proper army (despite secret appeals to Catholic Spain), was forced to recall the exiled Parliament. They immediately attacked the King's administration, but Charles made it clear he would reverse any concessions.

By the end of 1641, Parliament was forced to adopt a more radical hard-line approach, championed by John Pym and John Hampden. The king was now considered so irresponsible that Parliament, on the people's behalf, was obliged to adopt more power. Fearing a turnabout in religious attitudes, Catholics in the north of Ireland attacked new Protestant settlers from England who might support this new radical Parliament; they claimed to act on the king's authority. Many Protestants were killed in one of the worst British civilian massacres in history. Obviously Charles could not be trusted to defend the Protestants and he was accused by the hard-liners of being a deranged king. On 20 August 1642, Charles raised his standard at Nottingham and declared war on Parliament.

For many the division of loyalty was too great. Most families in Stamford probably kept their heads down and tried to stay out of the conflict. There seems to have been no widespread support for either of the religious parties, Puritan or Laudian. John Vicars of St Mary's Church had been put on public trial and humiliated in 1631 for his extreme Puritan views. The tradition of loyalty lay with the Crown and Established Church, and although this loyalty was sorely tested by Charles I's actions, it probably held sway. A visit by Charles to Stamford in 1632 had prompted a practically bankrupt council to offer gifts of silver. However, the general impoverishment of the town prevented a great display and the second Earl of Exeter complained that they had failed to entertain the king fittingly. Two of the leading local families were Royalist: the Noels (third Viscount Camden) at Exton Hall and the Berties who had inherited Grimsthorpe Castle from the Willoughby de Eresby family; Robert Bertie, first Earl of Lindsey and general in the king's army, was killed in 1642 at the Battle of Edgehill. They must have supported Stamford's Royalist MP, Geoffrey Palmer.

As John Cecil, the fourth Earl of Exeter, was in his minority at the outbreak of war, the political position of the Cecil estate is more difficult to assess. Traditionally the family were Anglican Protestant, but was their dislike of Charles I's Laudian reforms strong enough for them to oppose the Crown? Certainly the Hatfield branch of the family sided with Parliament, and the Grey family, who had inherited the manor of Stamford from the Cecils, played an active role for Parliament during the war. Furthermore, Stamford's second MP, Thomas Hatcher from Careby, was a Parliamentarian and we know that the Cecil/Grey interest supported the Hatchers in the election of 1676. On the other hand Royalist forces used Wothorpe and Burghley as defensive positions and after the war the second Duke of Buckingham came to live at Wothorpe after his house at Burley-on-the-Hill, nine miles west of Stamford, was destroyed by Parliament. It is probably fair to say that, apart from the siege of 1643, the Cecils kept out of the war and so avoided any painful choices.

The siege of Burghley occurred in the summer of 1643. The victory of Royalist forces from Belvoir and Newark at Ancaster Heath prompted a southern offensive led by Viscount Camden of Exton. After defeat at Peterborough on 19 July, Camden retreated to Stamford and occupied his cousin's house at Wothorpe, which was hastily fortified. Time was against them. Oliver Cromwell's swift arrival from Northamptonshire forced the Royalists to move to the Cecils' main house at Burghley, where, following the arrival of Parliamentary reinforcements on 24 July, a siege began. Camden's army was heavily outnumbered and, fearing damage to the house, he surrendered the following afternoon. Apparently the churches in Stamford had rung their bells backwards to summon Royalist support. Certainly many of the rectors had Royalist sympathies, for when churches were cleared by Parliament of Royalists in 1645, all the rectors north of the river were removed; the national proportion of ejections was nearer one in five.

Stamford suffered throughout the war from the continual comings and goings of troops on both sides. About one in ten of all adult males was in arms and each side demanded free quarters for its soldiers. High taxation and high food prices led to economic recession and towns like Stamford were barely able to cope.

Gradually, Parliament's well-paid and well-organised New Model Army gained the upper hand. Charles I was forced to flee from his stronghold at Oxford and at the beginning of May 1646, he took refuge in Stamford at Blackfriars, the house of the Cave family, which stood off Wharf Road outside the town walls. He did not stay in Barn Hill as is traditionally believed; Michael Hudson, the king's companion, testified that the 'King was at noe gentleman's house but Mr Cave's in Stamforde'. He stayed one day and then rode to Southwell where he surrendered himself to the Scottish army in expectation of their support. Instead they sold him to Parliament for £400,000 and the first Civil War ended.

In 1647, another national purge removed almost half of Stamford's burgesses for Royalist sympathies. But a settlement with Charles and a solution to the political problems became increasingly remote. Charles had initially led Parliament to believe that they could negotiate with him, but on 11 November 1647, he escaped and signed a secret agreement with Scotland. This sparked off Royalist uprisings in spring 1648 which began the Second Civil War. In June a Royalist rebellion began at Stamford led by the king's servant, Dr Michael Hudson, the former rector of nearby Uffington, the Reverend Thomas Stiles of Crowland and leading Stamford Royalists such as Richard Wolph. Following its suppression at Woodcroft House, near Etton seven miles east of Stamford, a further purge of the Corporation was made. The Second Civil War ended with the Treaty of Newport which was signed by Charles and the Presbyterian wing of Parliament. But the Army General Council refused to accept the treaty and on 6 December 1648 they purged the House of Commons of MPs who had favoured the negotiated settlement.

The king had fought a civil war and lost. His duplicity had alienated many people from his cause and the Army and Parliament had no option but to put the king on trial for treason in waging war on the kingdom of England. John Weaver, a radical Parliamentarian from North Luffenham, who replaced Palmer as MP for Stamford in 1645, was one of the 135 members appointed to try the King. Like many others he refused to sit in judgment and only 59 members of the court actually signed the death warrant. On 30 January 1649, Charles was executed in Whitehall in London; the monarchy and the House of Lords were abolished and a Commonwealth was declared.

But Charles' martyrdom was his finest moment; the Commonwealth led by Oliver Cromwell and the Army would never achieve more than minority support. The Scots were particularly outraged and in 1651 they supported Charles II in a bid to restore the monarchy which ended with defeat at the Battle of Worcester. Despite the reduction of Parliament to a radical hardcore (the Rump Parliament), attempts to govern were doomed by lack of consensus. Ironically, Cromwell was forced to abolish Parliament and rule alone as Protector. Although his foreign policy was highly effective, support at home remained fragile and repression became the rule of survival. Cromwell's death in 1658 left the country with no legal civil government and no leader: his son Richard was incapable and Parliament and the Army were divided. The Protectorate collapsed and the Civil War came full circle. Troubles over the last 20 years and the lack of any positive leadership meant that a restoration of the monarchy became inevitable.

Opposite: *Tower of St George's Church, rebuilt in the late 17th century*

ROADS
TO PROSPERITY

IN 1660, Charles II took the throne, but the power of the new monarchy was regulated. Parliament retained most of the legislation that Charles I had ratified between 1641-2. In addition taxation could not now be levied without the consent of the House of Commons and Parliament assumed supremacy over the restored Church of England so that churchmen like Laud could not hold senior political office. On the other hand, the king was given back command of the army. Cromwell's supporters were removed from official positions: Stamford Corporation was purged in 1662 and burgesses who had replaced Royalist sympathisers in the 1640s were themselves displaced. And the new relationship between Parliament and the Church excluded Puritans: Dissenters were barred from holding political and other key positions.

Those faithful to the Royalist cause flourished at the expense of Dissenting or neutral gentry. The Bertie family of Grimsthorpe and the Noel family of Exton were typical. Robert Bertie, third Earl of Lindsey, began courting royal favour with the political rise of his brother-in-law, the Earl of Danby, architect of Charles II's attempted centralised political system. The Bertie ascendancy began with them gaining one of the Stamford seats in the Restoration Parliamentary election. Then, in 1673, Charles Bertie, the youngest son, bought an estate at Uffington, two miles to the east of Stamford. Three years later the Cecil-backed Stamford MP resigned and in the following by-election the Court Party candidate, Henry Noel, beat the Cecil-backed Hatchers of Careby. In December the same year Viscount Camden (a Noel) replaced John Cecil, fourth Earl of Exeter, as Recorder for

Above: *Bull & Swan, High Street St Martin's, built around the mid 17th century*
Opposite: *Nos. 13-15 All Saints' Street display a variety of late 17th-century bays*

the town and Charles Bertie replaced Noel as MP on the latter's death in 1677. The Berties consolidated their successes by presenting a silver mace to the Corporation. The Cecils, at least for the time being, appeared complacent. They were probably Country Party supporters. This was a political faction mainly made up of small landowners, the so-called squirearchy, but it included a number of large landholders, such as the Cecils, who believed in decentralisation and non-intervention. With the succession of John, fifth Earl of Exeter, in 1678, this aloofness continued with an Earl who was more interested in foreign travel and art than politics; he was responsible for the Baroque remodelling of the interior of Burghley House, complete with painted walls and ceilings by Antonio Verrio.

The 'Popish Plot' to depose Charles and put his Catholic brother James on the throne accentuated suspicions about the government. Danby was imprisoned in the Tower and the Earl of Shaftesbury and the Country Party united to oppose Court rule. In Lincolnshire these events were combined with the political battle between Sir Robert Carr and the Berties. The immediate result was victory for Cecil- and Carr-backed candidates in the 1679 and 1681 Stamford elections. But Court influence was too strong. Sir Robert Carr died in 1683 and on the accession of James II in 1685, the Berties retook both Stamford seats, offering a huge punch bowl to the Corporation so that '...the citizens of Stamford may celebrate their fidelity towards the most serene kings of Great Britain, then their friendship to the house of Bertie'. The Berties also secured a charter for the town which augmented one passed in 1663. Uffington House and Grimsthorpe Castle were rebuilt and the family

were wealthy enough to employ Sir John Vanbrugh to further alter Grimsthorpe in the early eighteenth century. But James II was a Catholic. He granted full religious liberty to Catholics and appointed a Catholic as Lord Lieutenant of Ireland. When soldiers from Ireland began to arrive in England, memories and fears of 1641-42 were revived. What followed was a coup in which James' Protestant daughter, Mary, and her Dutch husband, William of Orange, were invited by Parliament to come to England to take the Crown. James' supporters deserted him: Danby and the Berties quickly swapped sides and rallied to William.

The so-called 'Glorious Revolution' of 1688 placed William and Mary jointly on the throne. It also clarified the government of the country: the king could not be a Catholic; he could not suspend the law; he was dependent upon Parliament to vote money for government; the king's ministers were answerable to Parliament and no royal pardon could overrule the will of Parliament. The Berties maintained their Stamford seats in a display of loyalty to the new king. The fifth Earl of Exeter, however, was initially reluctant to support William, but by 1698, the Cecils had formed a political alliance with the Tory Bertie and Noel families. This shifted slightly when in 1705 Robert Bertie, fourth Earl of Lindsey, declared himself a Whig; he prospered under Whig rule and was created Duke of Ancaster by George I. The Cecils continued the alliance with Charles Bertie of Uffington. A political system that could allow for different interpretations of the nature of power via the two new political parties (Tory and Whig) is perhaps the longest-lasting political legacy of the seventeenth-century constitutional struggle. The Cecils' shift from the Country Party to an anti-ministerial position allied with the Tory Party was a significant moment for the political future of Stamford. As the Whig Party developed out of the Country Party it became more and more concerned with the privileges of Parliament and the rights of its members; it was to dominate politics throughout the first half of the eighteenth century. The Tory Party lost its close relationship with the king and remained alienated from the national political scene for over 50 years.

There was little joy for the Dissenters. The Toleration Act of 1689 still excluded them from political office, although they now had the right to worship in their own buildings. However, in 1714 the Presbyterian Chapel in St Paul's Street, Stamford, was burned to the ground in a riot; it was rebuilt six years later in Star Lane. Stamford was a bastion of the Established Church: in 1704, there were only 17 Dissenters or Nonconformists recorded in the town out of a total population of over 2000. The absence of Dissent and the decline of Church influence combined with growing wealth to create a more leisure-orientated society. London was the cultural centre of this development, but Stamford, on the Great North Road, became one of the first provincial towns to stage plays (from 1698), to hold dances in assembly rooms and to have a racecourse.

Stamford's close associations with lines of communication created the economic growth necessary for such a lifestyle. In 1664, Daniel Wigmore, a wealthy woollen draper, bravely took on the construction of the beleaguered Welland Navigation canal. He succeeded where others had failed and reaped the rewards by collecting tolls. The Welland was once

---

Opposite top: *Nos 11-12 St Paul's Street. No. 12 was refronted by the Norris family in 1663*
Opposite below left: *No. 12 St Paul's Street; detail of bay*
Opposite below right: *No. 32 St Paul's Street; an early example of the 'Stamford Vernacular' style*

again navigable to the eastern ports. At long last the town was able to transport, not only the local barley crop, but also malt producd in the town. An extensive malting industry developed, and in 1676 the Cecils built a new wharf off Water Street to cope with the trade. Stone and agricultural grains were shipped out in flat-bottomed barges; coal and groceries arrived in exchange.

It was the Great North Road, however, which was to become the lifeline of Stamford's new prosperity. After the Restoration, long-distance coach services became increasingly common. People were encouraged to travel as journey-times were cut by regularly changing horses en route. London was the main attraction: the city was rapidly expanding into the commercial capital of the world and people flooded into the metropolis in the hope of making a fortune or finding a job. During the eighteenth century the population of London rose from around 350,000 to over one million. Stamford, positioned midway between London and York, and only two days journey time from either, was ideally situated to take trade from travellers; as in medieval times a whole cross section of society passed through its streets. Much-needed road improvements came in the 1730s when construction and maintenance of roads passed from parish control into the hands of turnpike trusts which charged tolls; a nineteenth-century toll-bar cottage can still be seen at Newstead one mile east of Stamford. Muddy tracks became well-surfaced roads in a national network which further slashed travel times. By the middle of the eighteenth century, London was less than a day away from Stamford and stiff competition meant that stage-coach fares were lower than ever.

Changing horses for stage coaches meant that stabling and accommodation facilities were required. This is when the coaching inn began to evolve. Old travellers' inns like the George, and the George and Angel (formerly the Angel of the Hoope) and the Bull in St Mary's Street, adapted themselves to the new trade. The front range of the George was rebuilt in 1724 by the Cecils, and the writer Daniel Defoe stopped there 'out of curiosity, because it is reckoned one of the greatest Inns in England'. New inns opened up: the Falcon

Above: mid 18th-century warehouses lining the river by the Town Bridge
Opposite: No. 19 St George's Square; built in 1674, this was the first Classical house in Stamford

and Woolpack in St Martin's (now the Bull and Swan) and later inns, such as the mid-eighteenth century Coach & Horses and Waggon & Horses in St Martin's, bear witness to the new traffic.

As in other towns across the country, shops and service-industries developed. Market stalls and shambles filled High Street and Red Lion Square and small shops, in the modern sense, began trading from the ground floors of houses. Cutlery, ceramics, soaps, teas and coffees, chocolates, medicines, silks, rich damasks, French brandies and wines were just some of the products on offer. Stamford was a perfect example of economist Adam Smith's notion of England as a new 'nation of shopkeepers'. But Stamford was not just a service-station for refuelling travellers; it was also the commercial centre of the region. By 1714, the town staged six major fairs and four large cattle markets each year. Agriculture advanced dramatically with the emergence of efficient capitalist farmers; enclosure of land and fen drainage increased crop production and Stamford benefited from the sale of produce in its streets and shops. Small workshops manufactured such things as cabinets, watches, clocks, leather products and textiles, all of which could be delivered by carriers to surrounding villages, while printers, builders and apothecaries offered wide-ranging services. Gentlemen and prosperous farmers coming into town for business or shopping also stopped to take professional advice from bankers, lawyers, doctors and estate agents. Perhaps they brought their families and stayed on to watch a play or attend a dance. They might also have sent their children to one of the many new private schools.

This concentration of business and consumer interests, combined with the removal of press censorship in 1695, encouraged William Thompson and Francis Bailey to set up a

Opposite: No. 12 Barn Hill; detail of doorway c. 1700
Above: The rendered range (Nos. 14-17 High Street) dates from c.1700

regional newspaper in the town. The *Stamford Poste* was launched in 1710, but was reduced in size and renamed the *Stamford Mercury* following the restrictive Stamp Act two years later. It concentrated on national issues and became the East Midlands' main regional newspaper up to the late nineteenth century.

Money was once again coming into the town. In spite of repeated outbreaks of smallpox, the population began to rise for the first time in four centuries; by 1801, the date of the first census, the population had doubled to around 5,000. The growth of services and marketing reflected a general shift in wealth towards the middle classes and it was this social group who dominated house building in Stamford through the Georgian age.

The roots of the new style emerged in the second half of the seventeenth century. The first houses to reflect the new prosperity developed earlier seventeenth-century vernacular traditions. They featured angled and gabled bays but, as at No. 32 Broad Street, they displayed a new symmetrical elegance enhanced by quality workmanship of the local limestone. Stone was now being quarried in Stamford and at the famous quarries at Ketton, Clipsham and Weldon. The new houses also featured Collyweston slate roofs instead of thatch. These stone slates were quarried at Collyweston and Easton-on-the-Hill just to the south-west of the town. Five of these houses are dated and only one, No. 44 St Mary's Street of 1656, is pre-Restoration. Then in 1674, Classicism arrived in Stamford. Daniel Wigmore, the canal builder, asked the architect of Lyndon Hall to design a fashionable town residence at No. 19 St George's Square, based on ideas first introduced into the area at Thorpe Hall near Peterborough. It heralded the arrival of the age of proportion and good manners which was to continue in house design until the 1830s; the travel writer Celia

Above: No. 3 All Saints' Place (the central house of 5 bays) dates from 1716
Opposite: The main range of the George Hotel was rebuilt in 1724 by the Cecil family

Fiennes described Stamford in 1697 as 'as fine a built town all of stone as may be seen... much finer than Cambridge'. A three-storey terrace range, built in the new style around 1700 at Nos. 14-17 High Street, was one of the largest secular building projects the town had seen. Other examples quickly followed, such as the elegant town house at No. 3 All Saints' Place of 1716, but this early simplicity soon gave way to vigorous rustication as local masons and builders interpreted designs from national pattern books. Both scale and composition, however, remained modest and provincial. There were no grandiose squares or terraces in the metropolitan manner; Barn Hill House, set in its own walled gardens, was the only building to display any real pretension. Where money was short, old medieval buildings were refronted or merely plastered over and Classical features imposed onto them. Stamford's middle classes favoured certain areas such as St George's Square, Barn Hill and High Street St Martin's, with the result that social distinctions in the town became more pronounced; in the 1780s the sheepmarket was removed from the affluent Barn Hill to a lower class area next to the old castle.

Leisure amenities improved through the eighteenth century. A bowling green was opened just outside St Peter's Gate in 1712. In 1717, the sixth Earl of Exeter laid out a racecourse on Wittering Heath, two miles south of the town. It had a straight mile as good as at Newmarket and Doncaster and attracted gentry from all over the East Midlands. An arcaded grandstand was added in 1766. In 1725, the eighth Earl built an octagonal cockpit capable of holding 500 people next to the George Inn. Two years later, Stamford got one of the first provincial assembly rooms in the country, built by dancing master Askew Kirk. Here, in refined surroundings, the respectable society of the town were able to dance, listen

to concerts and perhaps meet their future partners. Plays continued to be performed at the Guildhall in St Mary's Place until 1768, when a new theatre was opened in St Mary's Street 'after the manner of the London Theatres... [and] reckoned the completest place of its size in the Kingdom'. A subscription library was set up and there were numerous coffee-rooms and billiard-rooms. For the poor, traditional pursuits continued: there was an ever-growing number of public houses and beer houses, and the old bull-running festival in November acted as safety-valve for general frustrations and discontent.

However, the eighteenth century saw little improvement for the poor. Commercially, the main growth areas were connected with export trade to the new colonies in North America. Bristol, Liverpool and Glasgow became the country's major ports, revealing the shift of the country's industrial base from the South and East to the West Midlands and the North West. The corruption of government under the Hanoverian kings (George I, 1714-1727, and George II, 1727-1760) emphasised the gulf between the excesses of the rich and the desperation of the poor. Sir Robert Walpole and Henry Pelham led a notorious Whig administration which presided over such fiascos as the collapse of the South Sea investment company in the 1720s. The greed and immorality of the rich soon became the subject of the scathing pen of the caricaturist. Attempts were made to improve conditions for the poor in Stamford but they did little to relieve the distress. Poor relief escalated to become a major expense, as it did in most parishes in the country. The water supply was again improved so that disease became less widespread, and in 1722 four doctors opened a public bath house near the river in the interests of common hygiene (although admission was by subscription). In 1700, Thomas Truesdale, a wealthy Stamford lawyer, endowed an almshouse in

Scotgate, but this housed just six poor men. Some private almshouses, however, were quite effective. George Williamson, a wealthy grocer, set up a small unpretentious almshouse in St Peter's Street in 1763, which by the end of the century provided more accommodation than the flamboyant Browne's Hospital. By 1739, Stamford Corporation was forced to address the problem of poverty. They converted Brazenose House in St Paul's Street into a town workhouse. Later, in 1770, the Corporation gave land by St Peter's Gate so that the mayor, John Hopkins, could compensate for a personal scandal by building an almshouse for poor married couples. In 1795, they built sixteen single-room back-to-back houses in Scotgate to rent to the poor. The Corporation also made efforts to provide education; in 1704 they helped set up a Bluecoat School in St Paul's Street which provided tuition for about 30 poor pupils.

Poverty existing side by side with middle class prosperity was a recipe for crime. Theft and poaching became common, and highway robbery, as immortalised by Dick Turpin, was a real threat on the Great North Road. In the absence of a police force the only deterrent to crime was outrageously severe sentences. In 1704, Cassandra King was hanged from the gallows off Little Casterton Road for burglary at Wothorpe. Riot was commonplace, but was tolerated so long as it acted as a safety-valve. However, national demonstrations in the 1760s in support of John Wilkes's radical agitation and the success of the colonies in the American War of Independence (1775-83) brought alarm to the Tory government of George III's reign. These fears were further fuelled by the anti-Catholic

Opposite top: *No. 21 High Street; a jazzy Palladian style building of 1732*
Opposite below: *No. 2 St Mary's Place; an accomplished town house in the pattern book style*, c.*1740*
Above left: *Window architrave at No. 35 High Street St Martin's*, c.*1740*
Above right: *Window architrave at No. 13 Barn Hill, 1740*

Above: *No. 23 St Mary's Street from St George's Square*

Gordon riots of 1780 and the outbreak of revolution in France in 1789. A backlash against popular gatherings and demonstrations began with the notorious St George's Fields massacre in London, where Wilkes's supporters were shot by Scottish troops. In Stamford, the 'rebels' riot feast', the bull-running, was attacked by the Corporation, supposedly on the grounds of cruelty to animals. In 1788, the Corporation under the auspices of the ninth Earl of Exeter claimed that the bull-running was a 'disgrace to religion, law and nature' and those involved should be punished by death. Troops were brought in to quash the festival but the attacks only hardened the resolve of the participants. John Drakard's *Stamford News* of 1819 criticised the hypocrisy of the objectors:

> Away then, with this spurious feeling and bastard humanity! which froths and foams at one yearly indulgence of the lower orders, and sympathises with the daily and destructive enjoyments of the high and the wealthy [foxhunting]...

The Established Church found itself becoming alienated from the poor; in 1741, St George's Church stopped its bull-running subscriptions. Above all, the eighteenth century was the age of the antiquarian vicar who devoted more time to intellectual pursuits than pastoral care; Casaubon in George Eliot's *Middlemarch* is a good portrait. William Stukeley, who was Rector of All Saints' Church from 1730 until 1745, wrote his great works on Stonehenge and Avebury in Stamford and his druidic interests and intellectualism cannot have endeared him to the poor people of his parish. Francis Peck, Vicar of Goadby near Belvoir (Leics.), was another Stamford antiquarian who, in 1727, published a vast academic book on the early history of the town. It was the inability of the church to face the problems of society which pushed people towards Methodism. This was a movement headed by John Wesley which used outdoor preaching (illegal in the Established Church) to reach more people. The group broke away from the Established Church in 1795; nine years later a

Above: *Town Hall, St Mary's Hill, erected 1776*

chapel was built in Barn Hill, next to Stukeley's old house. Fifteen years later a new larger Congregational Chapel was built in Star Lane.

However, Dissent was not common in Stamford. Drakard's *History of Stamford* (1822) blamed 'that spirit of apathy (arising from the overpowering weight of aristocratical influence...) which renders religion and politics, art and sciences, almost unnoticed'. The eighteenth century saw the Cecils, or Earls of Exeter, together with the Noel family of Exton, achieve a monopoly of political control in Stamford. The alliance was known as the Confederacy. First, the Berties were ousted. Robert Bertie, first Duke of Ancaster, had declared himself a Whig in 1705 and had shifted his political interests to the Lincolnshire towns of Grantham and Boston. The Cecils and Noels continued an alliance with Charles Bertie of Uffington, but at the 1727 Stamford election, Brownlow Cecil, the eighth Earl, ran two candidates and took both seats. The next contested election of 1734 saw the threat of Whig opposition from the Cust family of Blackfriars House, who were kinsmen of the Custs of Belton House near Grantham. The full weight of Cecil Tory influence was brought to bear upon the town. Thomas Hurst, Cecil's steward, was conveniently elected mayor in the run up to the election and used his influence over the Corporation and in the appointment of parish officers. Francis Howgrave, who took over the *Stamford Mercury* in 1732, probably received financial inducements to produce a newspaper loyal to the Cecil cause. Cecil bribery and intimidation increased. The parish registers were tampered with and when Cecil supporters from St Martin's (which was outside the borough franchise) and surrounding villages flooded the town, some found that they were illegally entered in the parish registers and that their names had been added to the voting register. Two days before the election, a violent attack was made on Blackfriars House and 30 casualties were sustained in the Cust household. At the final election the Cecil/Noel confederacy

engineered a dubious victory. Cust complained that 146 Cecil loyalists had corruptly obtained the franchise while 37 Whig supporters had been omitted from the parish registers and so lost their right to vote.

Cust was bankrupt and Cecil domination was secure. There would be no more contested elections at Stamford until 1809 and Cecil authority continued unabated up to the second Reform Act of 1867 and even beyond. The interference of the Earls of Exeter became bolder. In 1737-8, Cecil's steward, together with the mayor and a mob of supporters, laid siege to Browne's Hospital in an effort to secure a Cecil candidate to the position of chaplain. In 1747, Brownlow Cecil bought back from the Grey family, or Earls of Stamford, the manor of Stamford. The manor cost almost £7,000 but it ensured Cecil supremacy.

The accession of the ninth Earl of Exeter in 1754 announced a period of extensive building work both at Burghley and in Stamford. The landscape designer and architect Capability Brown was employed at Burghley from 1756 to 1779. When, in 1775-6, the turnpike commissioners demanded the removal of the old gate and Town Hall from the north end of the town bridge, the ninth Earl helped finance a new Town Hall at the corner of St Mary's Place and Hill. The new terraces and crescents of Bath and Edinburgh

Opposite top: *No. 20 St Mary's Street; the window bay is late 18th century*
Opposite below: *No. 1 Broad Street; an early 19th-century refronting of an early 18th-century house*
Above: *Bottle Lodges, St Martin's, built in 1801 as the main entrance to Burghley House*

perhaps inspired further building projects. From the end of the 1770s through to his death in 1793, the ninth Earl built a series of large, plain three-storey terraces along St Mary's Street, St Mary's Hill and Ironmonger Street. They were designed by Lincoln architect Thomas Lumby, but their scale, severity and repetition were at odds with the traditional varied streetscape of the town. The scheme ended with the accession of the tenth Earl, later first Marquess of Exeter, who was deep in debt and more renowned for his remarkable marriage to Sarah Hoggins, a farmer's daughter from Shropshire. However, in 1796, he effected the enclosure of St Martin's and altered the course of Barnack Road to extend Burghley Park northwards towards the town. It was almost 100 years before the Cecils allowed a similar enclosure of fields north of the town. In 1801, the newly-elevated Marquess built a monument in stone to Cecil power. On the Great North Road just south of the town, an extravagant Elizabethan-style conceit known as the Bottle Lodges was built. Costing a colossal £9,000, it served to remind townsfolk and travellers of who was in control.

Opposite: *Entrance to Burghley Estate Office, Church Street, 1876*

POCKET
BOROUGH

BROWNLOW CECIL was only nine when in 1804 he became the second Marquess of Exeter. He died in 1867, the year of the second Reform Act, and the intervening years saw Cecil control tighten in the face of liberal reform. The traditional system had always been based on the agricultural and property interests of great landowners and on their paternalism towards their tenants and employees. The middle class 'shopkeeper' society of the eighteenth century presented little threat to this status quo. But the social implications of new technology and increasing industrialisation through the nineteenth century encouraged radical ideas; ideas of equality and electoral reform, of personal improvement and capitalist development, and a belief in organised religion outside the established church. These developments attacked the very heart of institutions such as the Cecil estate. The response of the second Marquess was to resist all reform, and his actions prevented Stamford from becoming industrialised. Victorian Stamford was a true pocket borough, a fossilised town pickled and preserved by constant intervention and manipulation.

The nineteenth century began with a direct offensive against Cecil domination, born out of economic frustration. Hardship and depression caused by the crippling Napoleonic Wars polarised politics into 'revolutionary' and 'loyalist' camps. Stamford's only substantial industry was malting and brewing. In order to compete with towns like Newark on the River Trent, it was vital that Stamford be linked into the Midlands and so the national canal network. In 1809, a London merchant, Joshua Jepson Oddy, offered his services as a Whig candidate in the Parliamentary election. He was supported by local bankers and, unexpectedly, by Gerard Noel of Exton who severed his family ties with the Cecils (Gerard was not a direct descendant, being a nephew of the unmarried sixth Earl of Gainsborough who died in 1796; his action was probably prompted by the Cecils forming an alternative alliance with the Berties). Oddy's arguments were based on the economic issues (he supported the proposed Stamford to Oakham Canal) and they highlighted the differing interests of the landowner and of those who lived by trade and manufacture. At the election the Tory candidates won with ease, but Cecil invincibility was shaken.

The Whig opposition began to organise itself for the next battle at the 1812 election. John Drakard's radical newspaper, the *Stamford News*, lambasted the Cecils and their interference in the town. Gerard Noel began building a vast hotel in St Mary's Street to serve as a centre of opposition and tenements were built in Scotgate (Protection Place) and High Street (Billings Buildings) to house people evicted from Cecil property for voting against the landlord's interest. The Whigs highlighted corruption in the town. Free education for poor children had become a rarity, as revenues from the Bluecoat School and Grammar School were scandalously embezzled by burgesses and masters; Thomas Blore's investigation into Stamford's charities, published in 1813, fully revealed the extent of deceit and fraud. Whig hopes were dashed, though, when Oddy was found to be a former bankrupt. He stood down before the election in favour of Noel, but the aristocrat did not command the popular support of Oddy; his interest in fighting the Cecils was probably just personal. The result was defeat for the Whigs and Noel's withdrawal from Stamford's political scene. Noel later became MP for Rutland and supported Tory policy in

Opposite: *Stamford Hotel, St Mary's Street,*
begun by Sir Gerard Noel in 1810 as a centre of political opposition to the Cecils

Above: *All Saints' Brewery, All Saints' Street, built by William Edwards in the 1820s*

Parliament. The next election in 1818 was hastily contested by two outsiders but the spirit of opposition had dissipated and they polled just 16 votes between them. The Cecils had weathered the storm. While the rapidly industrialising towns of the north moved towards reform, the south remained the dominion of the Tory landowner. In 1815, the Tory government gave in to pressure from the great landowners and introduced the Corn Laws; these kept the price of corn artificially high at the expense of the poor who had to pay more for their bread.

During the 1820s, pressure for Parliamentary reform increased. The death of George IV in 1830 at last gave the reforming Whigs the opportunity to take office. Large industrial towns like Manchester, Birmingham and Bradford had no Parliamentary representation while the 600 or so voters in Stamford elected two MPs. In the huge 'rotten borough' of Scotland just 4,000 or so electors returned 45 MPs. Whig interests in Stamford revived with the support of Richard Newcomb, the influential owner of the biggest newspaper in eastern

Above: Newstead Mill, an early 19th-century watermill situated on the River Gwash

England, the *Stamford Mercury*. A committee was formed with fellow newspaper man John Drakard and two weeks before the election Charles Tennyson, uncle of Alfred Tennyson the future poet, agreed to stand as a candidate. There was widespread support for reform: 10,000 people greeted Tennyson 'The Emancipator' on his arrival in Stamford, and on nomination day the mob destroyed all the hustings in the Shambles Portico apart from Tennyson's section. A skilful campaign where Whig voters used only one vote and 'plumped' for Tennyson meant that he only just failed to be elected. The second Marquess was startled; 30-40 tenants were evicted for voting against the Cecil interest. Mob violence against the Marquess increased; his coach was attacked in the town, he had an armed guard stationed at Burghley and according to Lady Victoria Leatham he put cannons on the roof of the house to defend himself against possible revolt.

At the reform election of 1831, Charles Tennyson secured a brief but historic victory. He beat Thomas Chaplin (of the noted Lincolnshire political family) to become the first Whig MP for Stamford; it was the first time that the Cecils had had to share Stamford's representation in over 100 years. Such was Stamford's notoriety that the *Stamford Champion* reported that two Russian noblemen were advised to observe the election because it would be an illustration of the 'greatest battle between the aristocracy and the people'. That the situation in the town was at odds with much of the country is shown by the fact that the Marquess had to spend a rumoured £14,000 on 'influence' at what was generally a 'dry election', that is one where there was no need to bribe the electorate with drink. George Eliot in *Middlemarch* mentions that the last unsuccessful candidate at Middlemarch 'spent £10,000 and failed because he did not bribe enough'. Bitterness and tension ran high and Tennyson fought a duel with Chaplin at Wormwood Scrubs for allegedly slandering the

85

Marquess.

Ironically, the 1832 Reform Act did little to alter the overall balance of power and the great landowners maintained their influence for at least another 50 years. In Stamford it actually destroyed possible opposition to Cecil control because the associated Municipal Corporations Act of 1835 brought the Cecil-owned area of St Martin's into the constituency. The Marquess's pocket borough was secure and it still returned two MPs, more than many larger northern towns. William Gladstone, the Prime Minister, was able to report as late as 1880 that Stamford was 'a Tory fortress which has been used, from time to time, to find accommodation for a wandering Tory official who had been rejected by some constituency that was weary of him'. Certainly, after the Reform Act Stamford seats were made available to cabinet ministers who had been promised office but had difficulty in finding a seat. These included Northcoate Stafford, Chancellor of the Exchequer, and Sir Robert Cecil, future Marquess of Salisbury and Prime Minister.

At the election the following year, Tennyson stood down, realising the futility of the contest. Captain Arthur Gregory of the Birmingham Political Union was persuaded to take his place but his attempt was doomed. The election was accompanied by great frustration; windows were smashed and pitched battles in St Mary's Street forced the arrival of the Peterborough militia. But threats of eviction and retaliation bludgeoned through another Cecil victory. Stamford, and Grantham, were the only Lincolnshire towns to return Tories

Opposite top: Stamford & Rutland Infirmary, designed in the Tudor-Gothic style by J. P. Gandy, 1826
Opposite below: Truesdale's Hospital, Scotgate, designed by George Basevi, 1832
Above: St Michael's Church, High Street, designed by John Brown, 1836

to the new Parliament.

In the reform of local government which followed electoral change, the Municipal Corporation Commissioners were surprised at the extent of Cecil influence in Stamford. It found that:

> The great majority of the respectable inhabitants are excluded from the corporate body; the freemen are excluded from any control over the local functionaries; and the political opponents of the Recorder [Marquess of Exeter] are excluded from the magistracy and council.

> Under this exclusive system, the administration of justice is suspected, the police totally inefficient, and the town property mismanaged; while the influence of the municipal functionary [Marquess of Exeter] in whose political interest the council is elected, the magistracy appointed, and every office is filled, so far from being exercised in promoting the local interests of the borough, is exercised to check the natural process of improvement.

The Municipal Corporations Act of 1835 removed many of the old corrupt practices. The new council, which increasingly featured Whigs and reformers, was made accountable to the commissioners; a police force was set up and in 1841 responsibility for amenities passed to a separate body of Improvement Commissioners. However, little had changed by 1839, for the Tithe Commissioner was able to conclude that the Marquess of Exeter's sovereignty over Stamford is 'a state of barbarous intervention and blindness, which resembles more an African dominion than an English and wholesome interference'. Cecil's agent, Jeremiah Clapton, was registrar of births, marriages and deaths, clerk to the Board of Guardians of the Poor Law Union, whose first chairman happened to be the Marquess, and later clerk to the Burial Board.

Cecil fears of the radical effects of industrialisation produced stubborn resistance to measures to improve the town's economic viability; Stamford was never linked into the Midlands canal and river system. However, for the first half of the nineteenth century the town continued to prosper. As in the eighteenth century, income was created by the coaching trade and the town's markets. The road system was dramatically improved in the 1820s by the development of new engineering and road surfaces invented by John Macadam and Thomas Telford. Coach design became more sophisticated and journey times were significantly reduced. By 1830, the coaching trade was at its peak and traffic through Stamford was so heavy that a bypass was mooted. Shops, inns and service industries thrived on the vigorous bustle generated by one of England's busiest roads. The town's markets remained popular: in 1819 the corn market in Broad Street was the fourth largest outside London. With money coming into the town the population soared. In the first half of the century Stamford's population grew by about 70-80%: in 1801 there were about 5,000 people on both sides of the river; by 1851 there were just over 9,000. Part of the expansion was industrial. The malting trade had diversified into brewing. Joseph Phillips began brewing beer in Water Street in 1789 and the family brewery flourished into the twentieth century. Hunt's Brewery opened just down the street in 1814 and continued until 1927, while All Saints' Brewery, set up by William Edwards in the 1820s, was later

Opposite top: *Rutland Terrace, Tinwell Road; a large Regency terrace, 1829-31*
Opposite below: *Lumby's Terrace, off Water Street; workers' housing of c.1840*

taken over by Melbourn's and is now a brewing museum. But the brewing industry was essentially conservative; by its nature it was the antithesis of a new style of manufacturing industry, championed by Robert Owen (who served his apprenticeship in Stamford), which required temperance, productivity and self-improvement. The other growth industry in early nineteenth-century Stamford was also rooted in the past: silk-spinning employed up to 500 women and children, but it remained a co-ordinated cottage industry with only small mills operating in the town. Other pre-1850 industry, such as iron-founding and agricultural engineering, was all small scale.

Private patronage, middle-class prosperity and a growing population resulted in civic and building improvements. In 1808, a grand portico was built in High Street as an entrance to a new combined market. In 1839 the corn market moved into a new arcaded hall in front of Browne's Hospital. When St Michael's Church on High Street collapsed during alterations in 1832, there was sufficient money in the town to finance a completely new church. And it was built on a grand scale, in the Early English Gothic style, and was proudly described in the *Stamford Mercury* as 'one of the most beautiful buildings in the Kingdom'. It was a symbol of a self-respecting community. The Stamford Institution founded in 1838 'for the dissemination of literary, philosophical, scientific, mechanical and other useful knowledge' also reflected this mood. It moved after just four years to elaborate new premises on St Peter's Hill, with a concert- and lecture-hall, museum, library and reading-room. Cecil patronage of the Institution encouraged the foundation of a more modest rival society, the Mechanics' Institute, which began meeting in 1841. The Marquess of Exeter also pumped over £3,000 into making Barn Hill House presentable for Sir Robert Peel and other ministers to stay in during Queen Victoria's visit to Burghley in 1844.

Other improvements were more directly practical. In 1824-5 a gas works was built by public subscription on the old tenter meadows off Wharf Road, so that streets, houses and mills became properly lit for the first time. The threat of typhoid and cholera prompted health measures. In 1828, a generous bequest by Henry Fryer, a wealthy surgeon, resulted in the construction of a Tudor-Gothic style hospital on the site of the Greyfriary. Nine years later the Cecils opened a new waterworks at Wothorpe. But most of these improvements only benefited those who could afford it; all too often the new water-closets of middle-class houses emptied into the working class's water supply. The poor did see some improvement. Money from Fryer's bequest allowed for the rebuilding of Snowden's Hospital in Scotgate in 1823 and in 1832 for the foundation of a new almshouse on Kettering Road for six poor widows. Truesdale's Hospital was lavishly rebuilt in the Tudor-Gothic style in 1832 to designs by George Basevi, but the massive cost (said to be £3,300) produced accommodation for only four more men. In 1815, the National Society education programme built a school for girls on Wharf Road and in 1833 the Grammar School on St Paul's Street was doubled in size by the addition of a new room. In 1821, a new Gaol and House of Correction was built behind the Town Hall, but this proved insanitary and had to be rebuilt in 1842. Finally, under the directive of the unpopular Poor Law Union Act of 1834, a workhouse was erected on Barnack Road which also catered for paupers from the surrounding area.

Another symbol of the progress of improvement was the suppression of the bull-running.

Above: *Stamford Institution, St Peter's Hill, designed by Bryan Browning, 1842*

The violence and brutality of this working-class festival were unacceptable to a new generation of middle-class moral reformers. In 1829, J. F. Winks published a sermon which claimed the custom 'resembled more a scene amongst the savages of New Zealand' (convicts were not sent to New Zealand because of the supposed savagery of the Maoris) and a letter to the *Stamford Mercury* in 1842 concluded that the bull-running 'suited ancient times and uncivilised persons, but is a disgrace to Englishmen of the nineteenth century, who boast the march of intellect'. The Marquess of Exeter was not one for championing the 'march of intellect'. For him the bull-running was a cherished product of the old threatened system, and at the 1831 contested election, Cecil candidates had paraded under a flag of a painted bull. The Society for the Prevention of Cruelty to Animals and some Nonconformist religious groups became involved. The growth of Nonconformism reflected the mood of self-improvement; in 1834 a Baptist chapel had been opened in North Street, supported by an eminent surgeon, J. G. de Merveilleux. In the end, though, it was the financial burden of policing the 1839 bull-running which finally extinguished this ancient custom.

Much of this improvement, though, was only skin deep. The main problem Stamford had to face was the lack of space for expansion. The Cecils had engineered an enclosure of the fields south of the town as early as 1796, extending their park in the process. But they had deliberately delayed the enclosure of the northern fields. They owned substantially less land to the north and west of the town and wanted to gain more property so that after enclosure this could be sold or leased to building speculators at a handsome profit. But the

91

reasons for delaying enclosure were not just monetary. In the new £10 householder franchise, election control relied on limiting the number of houses and so the number of voters. Furthermore, population pressures meant that the open fields off North Street had already been encroached on by a motley assortment of hovels, beer houses and brothels; by 1845, there were some 400 dwellings both there and in New Town off Empingham Road. If the franchise system changed to a common household vote, Cecil ownership of this land would encourage tenants' support.

The second Marquess, therefore, prevented Stamford from growing. Poor people were crammed into insanitary slum courts and multi-tenancy houses in back yards off the town's main streets. When any land became available outside the line of the old medieval town walls, it was allocated for middle-class housing. Rutland Terrace, an elegant late Regency group, was built on the site of the old bowling green; later, in the early 1840s, the Brownlows of Belton House planned an ambitious estate on their Blackfriars site. The building programme of Richard Newcomb, the Liberal owner of the *Stamford Mercury*, was equally middle-class. He transformed the far end of Scotgate into a monument of defiance to Cecil lordship, but his huge house, Rock House, and ambitious terrace did nothing to alleviate the over-crowding. When he built smaller houses in Rock Road they had to be perched on a stone arch built out from a quarry wall. Space was so tight that the new Union Workhouse was erected on an old quarry site bought from the Cecils which cost a fortune to infill, while the Baptist Chapel of 1834-5 encroached into the unenclosed northern fields. St Michael's School had to be started in a public house. Industry also suffocated. There was hardly enough space for housing, let alone for factories; any business that did develop was severely restricted.

What compounded the problem was the transport issue. In the ten years following the appearance of Stephenson's Rocket in 1830, nearly 2,400 miles of railway track had been laid down connecting London with Birmingham, Manchester and Brighton. The end of the coaching trade, the lifeline of Stamford's prosperity, was inevitable. But if the projected Great Northern Railway line from London to the North-East were to pass through Stamford then industry would be encouraged and enclosure might be forced through. Joseph Locke's original route of 1844 skirted the eastern edge of Stamford with a station at Newstead, but an alternative route through the fens and Peterborough had considerable engineering advantages and was enthusiastically advocated in Parliament. Despite pressure from the town, the Marquess of Exeter failed to actively support the Great Northern line, being fearful, perhaps, of the pace of reform associated with industrialisation. He was one of the protectionist, anti-free trade Tories who opposed the abolition of the Corn Laws in 1846; these issues were more important to him than the railway. In the absence of any strong case for Stamford, the choice was obvious: in August 1844, Peterborough got the main line and Stamford was compensated with a Midland Railway branch route which ultimately connected Peterborough with Leicester. However, the Midland line suffered serious delays due to opposition from both the Marquess of Exeter and Lord Harborough of Stapleford Park, just east of Melton Mowbray. The Marquess resisted the proposal to run the line along the north bank of the river through land owned by Earl Brownlow. Instead he fought for a route along the south side which ran through his own land. Eventually the

Opposite: *Stamford Midland Railway Station, off Station Road, by Sancton Wood, 1848*

Midland gave way and offered the Marquess an inflated £35,000 for the land and a further £5,000 to rebuild the Cecil-owned Town Bridge, for years the 'narrowest and most dangerous nuisance between London and Edinburgh' (*Stamford Mercury*). The railway's impact was deliberately kept hidden: it ran through a long tunnel under St Martin's and the station was picturesque and antique in style. The Town Bridge was completed in the following year, following many delays, but the Marquess had the audacity to reimpose tolls, which resulted in pitched battles between drovers and estate servants.

Many people in the town were bitterly disappointed at the loss of the Great Northern line. A Stamford deviation was put forward in 1846, and although the Marquess agreed to sell land and have a station on his property, he refused to negotiate on the price. The £600 per acre demanded by the Marquess made the line uneconomic and in May 1847 a Commons Committee rejected the deviation. At the general election ten weeks later, the Liberals, led by Newcomb, invited John Rolt, a barrister, to contest the seat. His battle cry was simply 'Rolt and Rail' and a pub in Scotgate, owned by Newcomb, was renamed 'Rolt's Arms' in his support. But Cecil interests proved too strong; Rolt was defeated and those Burghley tenants who voted for him were evicted. The *Stamford Mercury* claimed that many more people would have voted for Rolt if their vote could have been unobserved by the Marquess. Newcomb petitioned Parliament, and his claim that the Marquess had interfered with the voting was supported by 394 signatures. A Parliamentary committee investigated the allegations but it found insufficient proof apart from the evictions. The main Great Northern line through Peterborough and Grantham opened in 1852 and, with the threat of large-scale industrialisation removed, the Marquess actively supported a connecting line to it at Essendine, four miles north-east of Stamford. The station, built in 1855 on Cecil land in Water Street, was a homage to Elizabethan architecture and proudly displayed the Cecil coat of arms. It later served as the terminus for another Cecil-backed branch line to Wansford, six miles south of the town, which opened in 1867 but served no economic purpose.

Stamford's immediate fortunes were bleak. The coaching trade, the backbone of the town's economy for more than 150 years, collapsed; service industries were forced to close. Old coaching inns, like the George and Angel in St Mary's Street and the Coach and Horses in St Martin's, shut down. Like other canals, the Welland Navigation was hit hard. It was last navigated in 1863, following years of neglect, and with its closure Stamford lost its river access to the sea. Building projects failed. The Brownlows' estate on the Blackfriars was abandoned and Richard Newcomb's death in 1851 meant that his grand terraced street from the top of St Mary's Hill to High Street never got beyond the first two shops. In 1871, the theatre on St Mary's Street closed, followed two years later by the racecourse on Wittering Heath; both were the victim of competition from bigger theatres and racecourses, now easily accessible by train. Finally, Richard Newcomb's dream of building a non-sectarian school in the town, outside the influence of the Marquess, was thwarted. He left £20,000 in his will but this was contested by relatives who invalidated his last wish.

Although Stamford never got the railway it wanted, the Midland and Essendine lines did open up opportunities for industry. As in other local towns, most of this new industry served

Opposite top: Stamford East railway station, Water Street, by William Hurst, 1855
Opposite below: Rock House, Scotgate, built for Richard Newcomb, owner of the Stamford Mercury

the agricultural market. In 1845, the Cecils built a brass and iron foundry next to the gas works for J. C. Grant which produced mainly agricultural implements up to Grant's sudden death in 1851. Around 1848, Henry Smith expanded his agricultural engineering business (established 1837) and began the company which came to be known as Blackstone's. He opened the Rutland Ironworks in an old builder's yard off St Peter's Street and was sufficiently established to exhibit at the Great Exhibition of 1851. The following year he went into partnership with Thomas Ashby and the firm expanded into what little space there was on the site. They began producing portable steam engines and exhibited at shows around the country. Rail travel also enabled Hayes and Son's waggon and carriage company of Scotgate to exhibit nationally. They won government contracts and business prospered, but by the mid 1860s, the problem of space in the town forced the firm to find extra premises in Peterborough. Thomas Gibson's iron foundry and agricultural engineering firm in Star Lane also expanded. One company, however, was not agriculturally based. In 1858, John Marriot Blashfield, a London terracotta manufacturer, was encouraged by the Marquess of Exeter to set up in Stamford on the site of Grant's foundry in Wharf Road. Blashfield was obliged to buy clay from Cecil-owned pits at Wakerley, six miles south-west of Stamford, in return for investment in kilns and engines. Using the fine local clay, Blashfield produced a high quality terracotta ware which was used at Buckingham Palace and was exported all over the world. However, by the 1870s the market was demanding cheaper mass produced terracotta and in 1875 the company was forced into liquidation.

These new industries, hampered by lack of space and of immediate access to a main rail line, could not make up for the loss of trade brought about by the death of the coaching business. Population began to drop; some migrated to the thriving commercial towns of the north. In December 1866 the *Stamford Mercury* reported that over 40 people had left Stamford that month for work in the cotton mill towns. By 1861, there were 8,344 people in the town and this had dropped to 8,193 by 1871. Stagnation in the town is emphasised by the growth of Peterborough. In 1774, the *Gentleman's Magazine* described Peterborough as 'the smallest city in England and but indifferently built'; by 1851 its population had grown to 8,763, an increase roughly in line with Stamford. But then the railway arrived: by 1871 Peterborough's population had soared to 17,429 and by 1901 it stood at 30,872. Even the *Stamford Mercury* was under threat. Its monopoly in the East Midlands was gradually eroded by the foundation of new newspapers eager to take advantage of the abolition of the Stamp Duty or 'Tax on Knowledge'. Its role, like the town, was becoming increasingly provincial. Enclosure meetings were held but still the Marquess stalled; Newcomb called the whole enclosure issue 'a running sore'. Only the new cemetery was allowed on the northern fields and while the dead enjoyed plenty of space, the living were shut up in slum courts and unauthorised hovels. Meanwhile, the architect of the cemetery chapel, Edward Browning, rich from Cecil patronage, was able to build a mansion for himself (The Elms, now Priory School) on enclosed Cecil land at Wothorpe.

But on the eve of the second Reform Act, Brownlow Cecil, the second Marquess of Exeter died. With him went the pocket borough he had resolutely defended for the last 50 years. Stamford was about to wake up to a new era when first steps would be taken towards a greater equality.

Opposite: *Central Cinema, Broad Street, designed by George Coles, 1937*

TOWARDS
EQUALITY

THE SECOND Reform Act of 1867 radically changed the political situation in Stamford. It reduced the number of MPs representing the town from two to one, while increasing the number of voters from around 850 to over 1,000. Its effects were emphasised with the introduction of the secret ballot in 1872; this made intimidation much more difficult and threatened the Cecils' means of control. The election two years later was the first to be contested since Rolt's railway effort in 1847. The Stamford Liberal Association put forward M. C. Buszard, a barrister on the Midlands circuit. Although pressed to advocate the temperance cause, the chapel versus pubs argument, he fought the election purely on whether Gladstone (Liberal) or Disraeli (Conservative) should be prime minister. He lost by 146 votes and a riot broke out on announcement of the result. However, the next election of 1880 was influenced by Gladstone's campaign of speeches against Disraeli's imperialism. It brought success for Buszard and a historic victory for the Liberals in Stamford; it is perhaps ironic that Stamford's last MP was a Liberal. The 1884 Franchise Act removed Stamford's remaining seat and put the town into a larger South Lincolnshire constituency where the Cecils had less influence. Nevertheless, at the 1885 election the Stamford division, which included Bourne and rural villages, returned the Conservative candidate while Lord Burghley, the son of the third Marquess, was elected for North Northamptonshire which now included the St Martin's area. If Stamford itself actually became more Liberal, its grouping with Kesteven, then with Rutland in 1918 and with Spalding in 1983, has meant that the constituency has consistently returned Conservative MPs to Parliament.

At last agreement was reached over enclosure. Much of this initiative came from the new Marquess. The agricultural crisis of the 1870s, brought on by the arrival of cheap corn from America, meant that landowners like the Cecils suffered a marked drop in income; by 1885, the third Marquess had debts of £330,000, accentuated by an extravagant lifestyle. The estate was in need of income and as the Cecils now owned 1,000 of the total 1,598 acres to be enclosed, enclosure was a lucrative proposition. An Enclosure Act was put through Parliament in 1871 and became effective in 1875. Houses and factories could now be built on the old open fields north of the town and from then until the early 1980s virtually all new buildings in the town were put up outside the old town walls. Land was sold to developers and speculators, although the Marquess insisted on the provision of a public park or Recreation Ground on Hunt's Close beyond the Baptist Chapel. John Woolston, a local builder, laid out a red brick estate to the east of the Recreation Ground while larger, middle-class housing lined the Tinwell, Empingham and Casterton Roads and the east end of St Paul's Street. Industry was able to expand. In 1886, the company started by Henry Smith, now known as Jeffrey & Blackstone, bought a ten-acre site off Ryhall Road, adjacent to the Great Northern Essendine railway. Here they started producing the oil engines which were to bring the company great success in the twentieth century. In 1907, the Martin Cultivator Company moved from Blashfield's old Wharf Road factory site to bigger premises along Ryhall Road. Here they began producing a wide range of popular agricultural implements. Other industries were expanding. Hayes & Son, waggon and carriage builders, found a site on West Street and later bought the Rock Iron Works in Scotgate; by the 1880s they were producing some 300 carts and carriages per year. Williamson's brickworks off Little Casterton Road developed quickly in the first years of the new century. There was even an

Above: *Roman Catholic Church, Broad Street, designed by George Goldie, 1862-4*

attempt to establish a motor car business in the town. In 1903, a large factory was built in Gas Lane for the Pick Motor Company. It was partly financed by the fifth Marquess of Exeter and was soon one of the largest car manufacturers in the eastern counties. However, disagreements between the directors and John Pick, the engineer, resulted in its premature closure in 1906; Pick's later attempts at manufacture were all small scale. The development of industry was enough to boost the town's population; the first decade of the twentieth century saw the largest single increase since records began in 1801. The population rose from 8,229 in 1901 to 9,647 in 1911. However, enclosure came too late to make any large impact. A description of the town in *Stamford in 1892* reflected this:

> Taken as a whole, it seems doubtful whether Stamford will ever attain to any great degree of industrial supremacy. Both by Nature and the Railway Companies she has been left, to a certain extent, out in the cold. Nine residents out of ten… cling to the conviction that Stamford 'isn't in it' with Peterborough, or Grantham, or Spalding, and must forever remain as she is… Her people go their daily ways and say nothing, her council members maunder along and do nothing, and her men of money pile metal on end and give nothing.

The late nineteenth century saw the first steps towards greater equality in society. Governments finally recognised the appalling poverty and insanitary living conditions of the working class, while scientific and technological developments stimulated progress towards their solution. Stamford responded to national initiatives. Outbreaks of typhoid in 1868 and 1869 prompted a sanitary report and isolation wards were built at the hospital in 1879 in line with government recommendations. The town's drainage, sewerage and

Above: *Stamford School, St Paul's Street, extended and improved 1874-5*

water systems were renewed. The Education Act of 1870 stipulated that modern schools should provide basic education, which became compulsory in 1877. In Stamford, revenue from Browne's Hospital and the Grammar School was used to establish an elementary school (Browne's School in All Saints' Street) and two senior schools, one for boys, based around the old Grammar School on St Paul's Street, opened in 1875, and one for girls, High School in St Martin's, which opened in 1877. Here pupils were not only educated but disciplined to accept their place in society. The money from Browne's Hospital was donated following an investigation into corruption within the institution; in 1870, some of the revenue was used for rebuilding and improving the medieval almshouse. A national effort was made to remove corruption and increase professionalism in local services. Road tolls were discontinued. In 1889, County Councils were created and Stamford was put under Kesteven County Council; the influence of the town council waned as responsibility for decisions moved outside the town. The Stamford police service was disbanded. In 1894, a Technical Instruction School was opened in Broad Street by the Kesteven authority for education in 'art, science, hygiene and the principles of agriculture'. The cattle market was moved out of Broad Street in 1896 to a new home, away from houses, south of the river. Finally, the old workhouse was replaced in 1902 by a new building on Ryhall Road. Other improvements arrived. Telephones came in 1889, electricity in 1901-2 and old age pensions in 1908. A large new Post Office was opened in 1896. Meanwhile, the relationship between the town and the Cecils was changing. The family was in financial difficulty and huge amounts of land and property were sold off. The third Marquess had relinquished the despised tolls on the Town Bridge as early as 1868 and in 1882 he had sold his rights to collect tolls at fairs and markets to the town council. In 1909 a remarkable event happened

Above: *Stamford Football Club ground in St Martin's*

which epitomised the changing structure of society: the fifth Marquess was elected town mayor, the first Cecil to have held such a lowly position since David Cecil in the sixteenth century.

The last years of the nineteenth century also saw a sharp fall in prices which greatly increased the real wages of the working class. Between 1875 and 1900 prices plummeted by 40%. Birth control measures, perhaps prompted by rising material expectations, meant that families got smaller. Working hours were cut: in 1890 workers at Blackstones gained a reduction in the working week, although they still worked from 6am to 5pm Monday to Friday and 6am to 1pm on Saturday; early closing for shops in Stamford began in 1893 at 2pm on Thursdays. All this meant that the working class had more leisure time and more spending power. Watching and playing football became one of the most popular national pastimes and Stamford Football Club, nicknamed the 'Daniels', was formed in 1896 from an amalgamation of local clubs. They turned professional in 1910 and won the Northamptonshire League two years later (the ground was in Northamptonshire). In 1906, a public library was opened in the converted Shambles portico and an open air swimming pool was built in 1913. Cheap rail travel meant that day trips could be made to the seaside at Skegness or Norfolk, or people could go down to London to see a show or exhibition. Then came the cinema. In 1910, the Picturedrome was opened in the Odd Fellows Hall on All Saints' Street and by 1913 the Picture Palace was operating on Blackfriars Street. The cinema proved a great success by providing a refreshing escape from the mundane reality of life.

Self-help and self-awareness increased. A small Co-operative Society store had been opened in Red Lion Street as early as the 1870s and in 1901 a branch of the Peterborough

Co-operative Society was established in the town; this proved so successful that in 1909 a large store was built at no. 41 High Street. Popular tabloid-style newspapers were published to cater for the growing number of literate people. The *Stamford and Rutland Guardian* began in 1873 and the *Stamford and Rutland News* set up in 1912. Political aspirations came with the formation of the Labour Party in 1900; a Stamford branch was operating by the time of the time of the First World War. New awareness and prosperity filtered through into chapel building. A survey conducted at the time of the 1851 census suggested that only half of the nation's population attended church and, of those, half went to Dissenting or Nonconformist chapels. Dissent was not as strong in Stamford as it was in the North, but in 1865, a new Roman Catholic Church was opened in Broad Street; in 1886, the Methodists built a new chapel in Barn Hill and 14 years later the Baptist Chapel in North Street was rebuilt and enlarged. The established Church remained aloof: in Stamford large, exclusive rectory houses were built for St George's, St Michael's and All Saints' churches and St Mary's received an ostentatious Anglo-Catholic restoration in 1890 designed by J. D. Sedding.

Then, in 1914, Britain stumbled into war. Stamford's factories were turned over to war production. Hayes & Sons made ammunition carts and stretchers; Blackstones made shell casings; the Kitson Empire Lighting Company of Wharf Road made torpedo heads and Cuttings of Barnack Road made electrical dynamos for the Navy. By 1915, 1,400 men had enlisted from the Stamford area.

The social distress and upheaval caused by the war quickened the process of change. The old aristocratic system that the Cecils had epitomised was further threatened, yet it persisted in Stamford longer than in many other towns; in 1932, Carew Mildmay could still report that: 'In these shifting, changing, uncertain, anxious, democratic, demagogic days, Stamford is anchored... as a willing, deliberate, determined stronghold of feudalism.' Women over 30 got the vote in 1918 and universal suffrage followed ten years later. Under Lloyd George's reconstruction programme, Christopher Addison introduced the Housing Act, which was to shape family life and the appearance of towns for years to come. Local Authorities were now obliged to provide council houses and, by 1921 such houses were being built in Stamford along Melbourne Road and New Cross Road. As the new houses went up, so the old slum courts in the centre of town were demolished.

The war also burst the bubble of economic prosperity. Germany, America and Japan were now all competing manufacturing countries. In 1924, Hayes & Son closed down and the following year John Pick's resurrected car company finally died. Unemployment and strike action were common throughout the 1920s. Blackstone's were forced into short-time working and there was high unemployment in the Stamford area. The General Strike, which took place on 3 May 1926 in support of the miners, was a unique event in English history and seriously affected local industry. Extreme conditions bred extreme solutions and Stamford was the only place in the country where fascists were elected onto a town council. In 1924, Arnold Leese and Henry Simpson beat two Labour candidates and Simpson was re-elected in 1927, despite Conservative opposition. In 1929, the railway to Wansford was closed.

The 1930s saw little improvement. Population remained static at around the 1911 total but now there were over 1,000 people unemployed in the Stamford area. Job-creation

Above: *London Inn, St John's Street, rebuilt in 1939-40 as part of a traffic improvement scheme*

schemes were introduced and the site of the Norman castle was flattened to make a car park. Blackstone's, crippled by the fiasco of the Agricultural & General Engineering consortium, were on a three day week and in 1936 they were taken over by the Gloucestershire engineering company, Lister. The only good news was the continuing provision of council houses such as the Northumberland Avenue estate and the opening of Fane School in Green Lane for children of the new suburban residents. Cinemas continued to flourish by offering distraction from the hardship of recession; comedies and musicals proved very popular. But early cinemas were plagued by fire and when the Central on Broad Street caught fire on 4 March 1937 it was the third Stamford cinema to have burnt down in eleven years. However, George Coles of London, the famous cinema architect, was brought in and the cinema was rebuilt in the Art Deco style.

The year after the Central reopened, Britain was back at war. Stamford's factories were not vital for the war effort and so the town escaped serious bombing. Lister-Blackstone, who were making generators and machine tools, was the only significant target. In October 1940, a mis-directed bomb landed on Cornstall Buildings in St Leonard's Street; it never exploded. The plane then machine-gunned the Blackstones factory. Two years later, three bombs were dropped, but again they missed their target and hit houses in the Rutland Road area. There were no air-raid injuries but there were heavy casualties among local men in the 1943 North African Campaign. Meanwhile, money was raised for the war effort: £5,000 was collected to buy a Spitfire aircraft and during Stamford Warship Week in 1942 over £100,000 was raised. Railings were melted down for munitions as was the old

Crimean War cannon on St Peter's Green.

The end of war in May 1945 brought with it another period of reconstruction and restructuring. There was full employment in the area. Prefabs (temporary houses) were built in King's Road and council house building began again, this time in the Drift Road area. In June 1951, Stamford and the rest of Britain put the hardship of the post-war years behind them and celebrated the prospect of a new future, showcased at the Festival of Britain exhibition in London. In 1954, the Marquess of Exeter opened Stamford's 1,000th council house and by 1961 a third of Stamford's houses were council-owned. As people continued to move out of the town centre, old slums and terraces were demolished and pubs serving these communities, like the Welland Cottage, off Wharf Road, were closed down. They were replaced by new pubs, like the Northfields Hotel, which opened in the suburbs. In 1963, St Michael's Church closed down and a new suburban church in Green Lane was opened. Improved living conditions and good employment prospects resulted in an increase in population; by 1961 there were just under 12,000 people living in Stamford.

The progress made towards redistribution of wealth naturally put pressure on the old aristocratic families. The death duties payable on the death of the fifth Marquess in 1956 were crippling. Cecil property in Stamford was sold off and the character of the town began to change as manorial leaseholds gave way to private ownership. David Cecil, the sixth Marquess, was eager to avoid similar duties and offered Burghley House as a gift to the National Trust. But negotiations collapsed and instead the house and contents were put into a charitable trust. Parts of the house were opened to the public and, as elsewhere, this symbolised the end of the closed and rarefied world of the English aristocracy. Burghley House had become a tourist attraction.

Opposite: *The unspoilt town; looking down Barn Hill to All Saints' Church*

TOURIST
& RETIREMENT TOWN

IN 1955, the historian W. G. Hoskins wrote, in the *Making of the English Landscape*: 'but now that the human misery of the transition is over and forgotten, we may perhaps be grateful to the Cecils for the feudal obstinacy which kept the town from growing and preserved it for our pleasure today'. The absence of large-scale industry meant that Stamford had suffered no destructive redevelopment nor any significant war-time damage. Stamford was a preserved market town with a centre which still displayed the architectural aspirations of generations of its inhabitants.

This remarkable preservation has dictated the development of the town since the 1960s. The opening of the A1 north-south bypass in 1960 relieved the town centre of traffic congestion. Stamford was promoted as a site for a new university; a Civic Society was formed in 1962, and when conservation areas were introduced in 1967, pioneering efforts by local planning officers meant that Stamford was at the front of the queue. Stamford became the first conservation area in Britain. With the historic centre now protected by stringent planning regulations, the town escaped relatively unscathed from the scourge of 1960s planning. Environmental improvements occurred: in 1972, traffic was banned from High Street and Ironmonger Street. Finally, as the Cecils sold off more of their property, so ordinary people were more able to influence the character of the town.

However, a continuing problem for Stamford was its ambiguous siting at the junction of four counties. Schemes of amalgamation into Rutland or a new county based on Peterborough had come to nothing. Under the 1974 reorganisation, county authorities were reduced in power and Stamford was placed in a new district, South Kesteven, which had its headquarters at Grantham. Ironically, Stamford lost the borough status which it had held since 1462 and all decisions were now made outside the town. The old town council became no more than a parish council with an advisory role.

Although the town has lost its administrative power, it continues to grow both in size and in terms of national importance. Since 1961, Stamford has experienced a 50% increase in

Above: *The making of BBC's Middlemarch; St George's Square*   Opposite: *Pedestrianised High Street*

population. It is now a large town of over 18,000 people. Its unspoilt character, recently publicised by BBC's *Middlemarch*, together with moderate house prices and excellent road communications, has made it an ideal choice to commute from or retire to. The decision to make Peterborough a new town has accelerated this process; Stamford has become a dormitory town just outside a large, modern, industrial city. The suburbs to the north of Stamford now extend for over two miles towards Great Casterton.

But, as in other historic market towns, this influx of population has put a great pressure on the old historic core. National property developers have bought almost every available space in the town centre for new housing, with most of it aimed at the retirement market. Old gardens have been built on. The garden of Torkington House, once owned by a prosperous nineteenth-century family of solicitors and town clerks, is now a modern housing estate. Industrial sites like Phillips' Brewery and Stamford East Station on Water

Street have been developed. Even the castle site, which had remained open land since the fourteenth century, was built on in the early 1980s. And all the houses have been designed with little regard for the traditional architecture of the town. An increasing population has encouraged the arrival of national retailers who have systematically gutted shops along High Street in an effort to provide efficient and modern shopping conditions. In 1982, St Michael's Church was gutted and converted into shop and office units; the 1989 edition of Pevsner's *Lincolnshire* called it 'an unsympathetic use and an appalling conversion'. Rising population has also brought the interest of supermarkets and other out-of-town retailers whose suburban stores threaten the economic viability of the old town centre.

The commuter and retirement nature of the town has become increasingly apparent. Manufacturing industry has closed under the strain of economic recession. In 1974, Stamford's last brewery, Melbourne's, closed down after a century of brewing. In 1993, Mirrlees Blackstone shut down all engine production in Stamford and transferred operations to its Stockport (Cheshire) branch. Only the foundry and spares departments were kept open. Another producer of marine engines, Tempest Diesels on Foundry Road, went into liquidation, and in September 1993, H. G. Twilley Ltd., a textile firm founded in Stamford in the 1930s, was forced into receivership. Twilleys was bought up and continues in streamlined form. Stamford has been left in the 1990s with just one large manufacturing company, Newage International, who build electrical dynamos from their works in Barnack Road (formerly Cuttings and Stamford Electrical). Peterborough, on the other hand, has witnessed rapid industrial growth, particularly in the 1980s. The 'Peterborough effect' has eclipsed development in Stamford and enforced closures; the Central Cinema on Broad Street was shut in the 1980s and people in the town now have to drive to a multi-screen movie complex on the far side of Peterborough.

The future development of the town probably lies in tourism and light industry. The town's proximity to the A1 means that Stamford is ideally located both for tourists and small industry. Melbourne's Brewery is already a museum. There are many attractive stone villages and towns nearby and the area is rich in country houses such as Grimsthorpe, Kirby and of course Burghley. Rutland Water, the largest man-made lake in Britain, is a thriving centre for watersports and recreation.

However, Stamford needs to improve its image. A proper traffic management system and effective conservation, along the lines of some European towns, are essential. Heavy vehicles need to be restricted. An imaginative car parking policy could create a traffic-free pedestrian-friendly environment in crucial central areas; Red Lion Square, Sheepmarket and St George's Square could once again become attractive public spaces. Of course Stamford does not want to be a museum piece, 'fossilised and moribund' as Hoskins called it in the 1950s. It needs to be a living town, aware that its appeal lies in its uniqueness. Peterborough provides excellent modern shopping facilities and pays the price with bland uniform shops and awful retail architecture.

Stamford must recognise its greatest asset and celebrate its beauty. Film directors have seen this. In 1993, Stamford was used for the BBC filming of George Eliot's *Middlemarch*; it was the most unspoilt Georgian town they could find. Stamford has been hailed as 'England's best stone town'. Let us treat it then with the respect it deserves.

Opposite: *Looking from St George's Square to the spire of St Mary's Church*

GAZETTEER
BUILDINGS & SITES
IN STAMFORD
& SURROUNDING AREA

THIS GAZETTEER is a selective guide to buildings and sites in Stamford and the surrounding area. It is arranged chronologically by century to support the main text; corresponding chapter titles are included for easy reference. Each site is numbered and there is usually a separate map for each century.

Buildings and sites are introduced in a standard order: monasteries, friaries, churches and chapels; public buildings; houses and shops; industrial and miscellaneous. They are also introduced chronologically. Some buildings, like churches which are altered and added to over many years, feature in several sections; these are cross referenced by century: e.g. C13 means look under 13th century, ST means look under Stamford section, SA means look under Surrounding Area. Buildings and sites mentioned in the surrounding area are always within 30 miles of Stamford; most are within 10 miles. Many are open or accessible to the public.

PRE–ROMAN
SURROUNDING AREA
1. FLAG FEN
Near PETERBOROUGH, Cambridgeshire
17 miles south-east of Stamford

Flag Fen is a working excavation open to the public. Originally thought to be a Bronze Age fenland village, latest research now indicates that the 'island' site was too wet for habitation. It might have had a ritualistic or religious purpose.

ROMAN
STAMFORD
1. ERMINE STREET & ROMAN FORD
Breadcroft Meadow, ½ mile west of town centre
The site of the Roman ford across the River Welland is marked by a stone monument; the Boudicca reference is spurious. North of the river, the line of Ermine Street can be traced leading towards Water Furlong and Roman Bank.

SURROUNDING AREA
2. ROMAN FORT & SETTLEMENT
GREAT CASTERTON, Rutland
2 miles north of Stamford
The defensive bank and ditch of the Roman settlement are clearly visible just off the road to Ryhall. Finds from the settlement, which included a 1st-century AD fort, can be seen in Rutland County Museum in Oakham.

9TH – 11TH CENTURIES
DANELAW
SURROUNDING AREA
3. PETERBOROUGH CATHEDRAL
PETERBOROUGH, Cambridgeshire
15 miles south-east of Stamford

In the retrochoir is one of the most important pieces of Anglo-Saxon sculpture in the country: the Hedda Stone, dated *c.*800. It has a pitched roof like a shrine and features standing figures of apostles in an arcade. Comparable work can be found at St Margaret's Church at Fletton, just to the south-east of Peterborough centre, where an early 9th century frieze is set behind the altar. *See also* C12*SA*, **1**; C13*SA*, **1**; C15*SA*, **1**.

4. ST JOHN'S CHURCH
BARNACK, Cambridgeshire
4 miles south-east of Stamford
Barnack was an important stone-quarrying village from at least the 10th century. Both Peterborough and Ely Cathedrals are built from Barnack stone and all the early medieval stone-work in Stamford is Barnack. The village has one of the finest 11th-century church towers in the country. Typical Anglo-Saxon long and short work at the corners and familiar decorative pilaster strips. Some of the windows have triangular heads. Of particular interest are two decorative panels carved with interlacing foliage. In the north aisle is a marvellous piece of Saxon sculpture depicting Christ in Majesty, *c.*1000-50. Nearby Castor also has fine pre-Conquest sculpture. *See also* C12*SA*, **7**.

5. ALL SAINTS' CHURCH
WITTERING, Cambridgeshire
3 miles south of Stamford
The church has a monumental 11th-century chancel arch, which Pevsner describes as being without equal in the area. Also long and short work at the angles of the chancel and nave.

6. ST ANDREW'S CHURCH
BRIGSTOCK, Northamptonshire
20 miles south-west of Stamford
The church has important and substantial Saxon remains. The base of the Saxon tower still survives

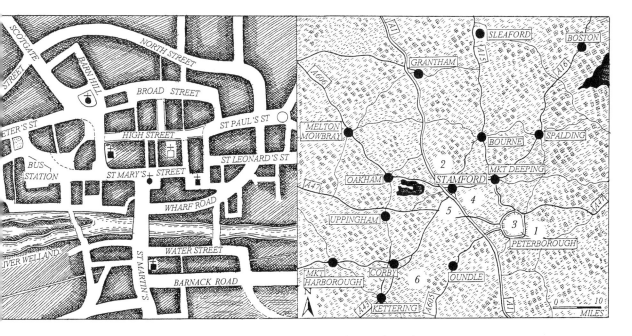

Above: *Buildings & sites from Pre-Roman times to the 11th century*

together with a curious and unusually large stair turret. The tower arch is reminiscent of that at Barnack.

12TH CENTURY NORMANS, CHURCHES & TRADE
STAMFORD

1. ST LEONARD'S PRIORY
Priory Road, ½ mile east of town centre

Tucked away on a grassy site near the river are the best Romanesque remains in the town. All that survives of the early 12th-century Benedictine priory is the nave and north arcade. Excavation has revealed evidence of a cloister to the south and a north transept and choir to the east. The highlight is the magnificent west front. This has an elaborate round-arched central doorway flanked by recesses and an arcade above with lancet windows in alternate bays. There is a large almond-shaped window in the gable (the Hospital of St John, now Cromwell Museum, at Huntingdon has a similar form). The arcade is supported on sturdy round piers. The priory was founded by Durham Abbey to manage its southern estates and later prepared students for study at Oxford University.

2. ST PAUL'S CHURCH
Stamford School Chapel, St Paul's Street

The remains of St Paul's Church are now incorporated into Stamford School Chapel. Fragments of the 12th-century church survive in the south-east corner. The arched corbel table, flat east buttress and sill frieze are the only 12th-century church fabric to be found in Stamford. *See also* C13*ST,* **4**.

3. STAMFORD CASTLE
Off St Peter's Hill

The bus station is built on the motte (defensive mound) of the Norman castle. The land drops away sharply on the south, or river side, into what was the bailey. This is now filled with modern housing. When the motte was levelled in 1933, the base of a round stone-built keep was found. For a better idea of a Norman castle go to Castle Bytham and Oakham. *See also* C13*ST,* **5**.

4. HOSPITAL OF ST THOMAS & ST JOHN
Lord Burghley's Hospital, Station Road

The hospital was built *c.*1170-80 on the river bank at the south end of the Town Bridge. A culvert to relieve flood water can still be seen. Above it are a 12th-century string course and buttress. *See also* C17*ST,* **2**.

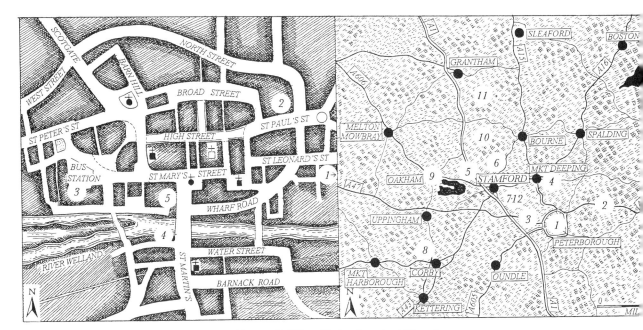

Above: *Buildings & sites from the 12th century*

5. No. 10 ST MARY'S HILL

This building incorporates the remains of a substantial stone-built 12th-century house, of similar date to the famous Jew's House in Lincoln. A mid 12th-century doorway with zig-zag decoration now leads into St Mary's Passage where there are traces of an undercroft arch.

SURROUNDING AREA

1. PETERBOROUGH CATHEDRAL
PETERBOROUGH, Cambridgeshire
14 miles south-east of Stamford

Peterborough has one of the most complete 12th-century cathedral interiors in Britain. Peterborough Abbey was a large Benedictine monastery built on an outcrop of limestone at the western fen edge. A disastrous fire in 1116 forced the Norman abbot, John de Séez, to rebuild the abbey. The chancel was probably completed by 1143 and the central apse of the 3-apsed east end still survives. The 4-bay chancel and 4-bay transepts share characteristics with Ely; both cathedrals have aisled transepts, an unusual feature in 12th-century architecture. The long nave of 10 bays dates from *c.*1150 onwards and is more conservative in design. Look also at the late 12th-century Outer Gate into Cathedral Square. The abbey owned the St Martin's area of

Stamford. *See also C9SA, 3; C13SA, 1; C15SA, 1.*

2. THORNEY ABBEY
THORNEY, Cambridgeshire
20 miles south-east of Stamford

Thorney Abbey, like the other fenland monasteries of Peterborough, Crowland and Ramsey, had considerable property interests in Stamford. All that remains is part of the 12th-century nave: the chancel, crossing tower, transepts, aisles and other monastic buildings have all disappeared. The original length was nearly 300 feet. The surviving nave fragment, however, is very impressive and similar in style to Ely Cathedral; the tall west front is comparable with the transept fronts at Ely.

3. ST KYNEBURGHA'S CHURCH
CASTOR, Cambridgeshire
8 miles south-east of Stamford

Castor has the most important 12th-century parish church in the area. It is also has a unique dedication: Kyneburgha was the daughter of Peada, King of Mercia, who founded Peterborough Abbey in the 7th century. The church has an ambitious plan with a magnificent central crossing tower and transepts. There is a rare dedication inscription, dated 1124, above a door into the chancel.

112

4. ST JAMES' CHURCH
DEEPING ST JAMES, Lincolnshire
8 miles east of Stamford

The church was part of a Benedictine priory founded by Thorney Abbey in 1139. It has an astonishing 12th-century south arcade.

5. ST PETER & ST PAUL'S CHURCH
TICKENCOTE, Rutland
3 miles north-west of Stamford

An unusual village church rebuilt in the 12th-century style in 1792. The interior is completely dominated by the original 12th-century chancel arch, wildly decorated with beakheads, green men, animals and zigzag. This leads through into a dark sexpartite rib-vaulted chancel which is very early (*c.*1160-70) and very rare.

6. ST MARY'S CHURCH
ESSENDINE, Rutland
4 miles north-east of Stamford

A diminutive church notable for its remarkable late 12th-century south door. This has a carved tympanum with a figure of Christ and two angels beneath a zigzag-decorated arch.

7. ST JOHN'S CHURCH
BARNACK, Cambridgeshire
4 miles south-east of Stamford

The late 12th-century north arcade has superb crocketed capitals comparable with those at *SA, 9*. See also *SA, 12*; C11*SA, 4*.

8. ROCKINGHAM CASTLE
ROCKINGHAM, Northamptonshire
18 miles south-west of Stamford

William the Conqueror built a castle on this early defensive site shortly after the Conquest; the steep hill made it ideal for commanding the Welland valley. It consisted of a motte and double bailey, as at Windsor, and parts of the 12th-century gate-house still survive. It was also used as a hunting lodge. Major repairs were undertaken by Edward I between 1276 and 1291 including the addition of semi-circular towers to the gate-house. The castle was later converted into a house. It is now open to the public. See also C17*SA, 10*.

9. OAKHAM CASTLE
OAKHAM, Rutland
10 miles west of Stamford

The 12th-century great hall is the best preserved early castle hall in England. It was originally built as a manor house with earthen defences. The hall is aisled with arcade capitals almost identical to ones in Canterbury Cathedral choir (begun 1175) and in Barnack church. The hall is open to the public.

10. NORMAN CASTLE
CASTLE BYTHAM, Lincolnshire
10 miles north of Stamford

The huge earthworks of the Norman castle dominate this quiet village. The great motte still survives surrounded by the ditches and banks of the bailey. These would have been topped with wooden walls and towers. In 1221, the castle was besieged by Henry III; despite heavy attack it held for almost 2 weeks. The fortification was substantially restored in the 13th century.

11. BOOTHBY PAGNELL MANOR HOUSE
BOOTHBY PAGNELL, Lincolnshire
15 miles north of Stamford

This is the most important small Norman manor house in England. The surviving building was the chamber or bedroom block of a much larger house defended by a moat. It was built around 1200. It has a vaulted ground floor with a hall and bedroom above. The massive limestone walls are up to 4 feet thick. The house is open by appointment.

12. HILLS AND HOLES
BARNACK, Cambridgeshire
4 miles south-east of Stamford

The old pits of the open-cast stone quarry create an incredible lunar-style landscape. The quarry was a major source of stone in 12th-century eastern England. It is now a nature reserve and there are many public footpaths. See also *SA, 7*; C11*SA, 4*.

13TH CENTURY
PROSPERITY & LORDSHIP
STAMFORD

1. ST MARY'S CHURCH
St Mary's Place

Superbly positioned at the top of a gentle hill rising from the Town Bridge. The tower is an outstanding example of 13th-century architecture.

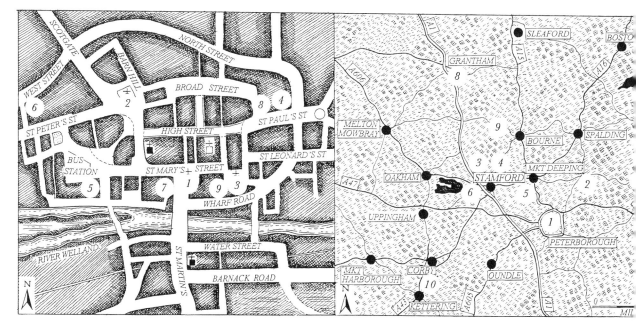

Above: *Buildings & sites from the 13th century*

It is decorated with layers of blind pointed- and trefoil-headed arcading culminating in a tall, elegant bell stage. Above the unusual west doorway are 3 roundels; the central one is decorated with a delightful interlacing knot pattern. Inside there is evidence that the church had 13th-century arcades of similar quality to All Saints'. *See also* C14*ST*, *2*; C15*ST*, *5*; C19*ST*, *7*.

2. ALL SAINTS' CHURCH
All Saints' Place
Although the church was completely rebuilt in the 15th century, it still retains its 13th-century core. The south and east walls have unusual 13th-century blind arcading at ground level. Inside, there is a spectacular south arcade of *c*.1230. The piers have multiple shafts topped with luxuriant stiff leaf capitals and the arches have multiple mouldings. The arcade is probably based on contemporary work at Lincoln Cathedral. The plain north arcade is slightly later. *See also* C15*ST*, *3*.

3. ST GEORGE'S CHURCH
St George's Square
The nave still retains its 13th-century three-bay arcades which probably date from *c*.1244. They look odd because they were heightened in the following century. The tower arch is also 13th century but was raised in the 19th century. *See also* C15*ST*, *2*; C17*ST*, *1*; C18*ST*, *2*.

4. ST PAUL'S CHURCH
Stamford School Chapel, St Paul's Street
Two bays of the 13th-century north arcade of St Paul's Church survive in the School Chapel. *See also* C12*ST*, *2*.

5. STAMFORD CASTLE
Castle Dyke
The great hall of the castle was rebuilt in the late 13th century and the screen passage doors still survive at the bottom of Castle Dyke. The mouldings of the arches can be seen from Bath Row. Just west of the Bath House, and set back, is another 13th-century doorway. *See also* C12*ST*, *3*.

6. 'BASTION' & TOWN WALLS
Petergate/West Street
This defensive tower is the only substantial fragment left of the late 13th-century stone town walls. It has an arrow slit and battlements.

7. No. 13 ST MARY'S HILL
This building was once an important 13th-century merchant's house. Steps led down from the street into a vaulted undercroft (built *c*.1220), most of which still survives. Here the merchant would

114

have sold his goods. Above, on the ground floor, was living accommodation; some early 13th-century wall arcading still survives there.

8. Nos. 12,14, 16-17 ST PAUL'S STREET

All these buildings originated as important stone-built 13th-century hall houses. This means that each house had a large single communal living and sleeping area open to the roof; a hole let out smoke from the fire. They still contain impressive remains: No. 14 has a section of an arcade and Nos. 16-17 have a two-bay wall arcade. Unfortunately nothing is visible from the street.

9. No. 17 ST GEORGE'S SQUARE

The remains of a thirteenth-century building are incorporated into a later house: there is a buttress and string course on the street front and at the side there is part of a blocked semi-circular arch.

BRAZENOSE GATE *See* 14TH CENTURY

SURROUNDING AREA

1. PETERBOROUGH CATHEDRAL
PETERBOROUGH, Cambridgeshire
14 miles south-east of Stamford

Peterborough has one of the most unusual cathedral west fronts in England. It has a monumental grandeur that is like nothing else in the country. It was added to the nave in the early years of the 13th century. It seems the original intention was to have 2 west towers with a front containing 3 portals, the central being the largest, as originally at Lincoln. However, after the north tower was built, the west end was further extended. A bizarre decision to make the side portals larger than the central one means that the extension bears no relation to the wall behind. It is topped with gables and pinnacles. Inside, the nave has an exceptional painted wooden ceiling of *c.*1220. In the precinct are the early 13th-century Abbot's Gate and the impressive remains of the Infirmary. *See also* C9*SA*, *3*; C12*SA*, *1*; C15*SA*, *1*.

2. CROWLAND ABBEY
CROWLAND, Lincolnshire
15 miles east of Stamford

This large and influential monastery is now a haunting ruin rising stark and bold out of the flat fenlands. The monastery was completely rebuilt during the 12th and 13th centuries. The main part of the west front is mid 13th century (but altered in the 15th) and similar in style to Westminster Abbey. It is adorned with numerous sculpted figures standing in niches.

3. ST PETER & ST PAUL'S CHURCH
GREAT CASTERTON, Rutland
2 miles north-west of Stamford

4. ST JOHN'S CHURCH
RYHALL, Rutland
2 miles north-east of Stamford

5. ST STEPHEN'S CHURCH
ETTON, Cambridgeshire
7 miles east of Stamford

Three churches substantially of the 13th century. Great Casterton has a remarkable 13th-century chancel with 2 lancet windows in the east wall; Ryhall has a fine 13th-century tower with contemporary broach spire (an even earlier spire can be seen at Barnack). Etton, however, is the most complete 13th-century church in the local area; isolated in the Fens it has escaped any significant alteration.

6. ST MARY'S CHURCH
KETTON, Rutland
5 miles west of Stamford

The 13th-century crossing tower is a slender version of St Mary's in Stamford. Pevsner says it is 'a tower that might be the pride of any county'. Like St Mary's it is topped with a 14th-century broach spire.

7. ST MARY'S CHURCH
WEST WALTON, Norfolk
30 miles east of Stamford

The finest 13th-century parish church in the country. It dates almost entirely from *c.*1240 and derives its influence from churches in Lincoln. It has a detached bell tower, a precaution to the dangers of subsidence in the marshy fens. The exquisite arcades are reminiscent of the south arcade of All Saints' Church in Stamford.

8. ST WULFRAM'S CHURCH
GRANTHAM, Lincolnshire
20 miles north-west of Stamford

Considered by Pevsner to be in the top 12 churches in the country. The church was largely rebuilt in the late 13th/early 14th centuries. The magnificent steeple rises to 282 feet, making it among the tallest in England.

9. GRIMSTHORPE CASTLE
GRIMSTHORPE, Lincolnshire
10 miles north of Stamford

The early history of the castle, which was built by De Gant, Earl of Lincoln, is linked with the neighbouring Cistercian abbey of Vaudey. Remains of the early 13th-century castle are incorporated into a later stately home: the large, square St John's Tower survives at the south-east corner. The house is open to the public. *See also* C18*SA, 3*.

10. GEDDINGTON CROSS
GEDDINGTON, Northamptonshire
20 miles south-west of Stamford

Only 3 of Edward I's 12 Eleanor Crosses still stand and this is one of them. The crosses marked the places where Queen Eleanor's funeral cortège stopped on its journey to Westminster Abbey in December 1290. The Geddington Cross is the most modest and best preserved of the surviving crosses. It is superbly positioned right in the village square. Stamford also had a cross (situated off Casterton Road) but it was destroyed about the time of the Civil War.

14TH CENTURY
BLACK DEATH, WAR & DECLINE
STAMFORD

1. GREYFRIARS' GATE
End of St Paul's Street
½ mile east of the town centre

The Greyfriary was the wealthiest of Stamford's 4 friaries. Only its gate-house survives. This was built *c.*1350 and has a 4-centred doorway flanked by buttresses topped with canopied niches. It was incorporated into a Porter's Lodge for the Stamford and Rutland Infirmary in 1848.

2. ST MARY'S CHURCH
St Mary's Place

The bold addition of a broach spire onto the earlier tower at St Mary's is the only great achievement still surviving in Stamford from this century. Soaring up to 162 feet, the steeple dominates the southern entrance into the town. The spire is adorned with sculpture and ogee-headed lucarnes. Also of the 14th century is the north chapel, which was built by the wealthy

Corpus Christi Guild. *See also ST, 3*; C13*ST, 1*; C15*ST, 5*; C19*ST, 7*.

3. No. 4 ST MARY'S PLACE
The site of the guildhall of Stamford's wealthiest trading guild, the Corpus Christi. It was later used by Stamford Corporation from 1462 until 1557 when a town hall was built. An ambitious late 14th-century rib-vaulted undercroft still survives beneath the 18th-century building. *See also ST, 2*.

4. No. 28 ST MARY'S STREET
Former St Mary's Rectory

A plain stone-built house probably dating from the 14th century. It has a cross wing to the east which contains a reset 12th-century window head.

5. No. 6 ST PETER'S HILL
The ground floor window of the gable end uses a decorated 14th-century string course as a lintel. The fragment probably came from the adjacent St Peter's Church (demolished in the 16th century).

6. BRAZENOSE GATE
St Paul's Street

Although the doorway dates from the 13th century, popular tradition associates it with events that occurred in the 14th century. This is the supposed site of Brazenose Hall, where Oxford masters and students attempted to set up a rival university in 1333. However, there is no medieval evidence of there being a college here. The door knocker is a replacement; the original is now at Brazenose College in Oxford.

SURROUNDING AREA
1. ST ANDREW'S CHURCH
HECKINGTON, Lincolnshire
30 miles north-east of Stamford

For 14th-century church architecture the best place to go is the area around Sleaford. Heckington is arguably the best 14th-century church in England. Its east window is a *tour de force* of flowing tracery. Inside is a superbly carved Easter Sepulchre of *c.*1330.

2. ST JOHN'S CHURCH
CORBY GLEN, Lincolnshire
15 miles north of Stamford

An excellent series of wall paintings dating from the 14th to the early 15th century. They include a giant St Christopher, originally almost 11 feet high, a Tree of Jesse, and nativity figures.

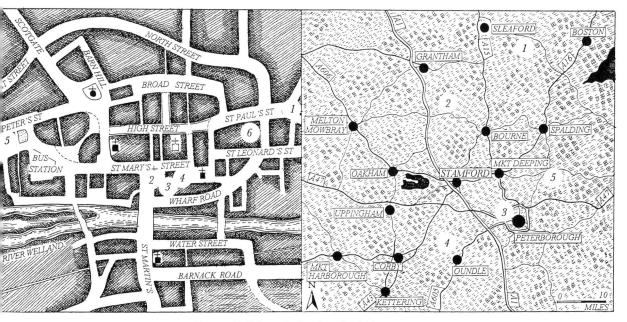

Above: *Buildings & sites from the 14th century*

3. LONGTHORPE TOWER
LONGTHORPE, Peterborough, Cambridgeshire
12 miles south-east of Stamford

A rare survival of a medieval manor house. The square tower was added to the late 13th-century hall in *c.*1300. The tower contains a series of unique wall paintings, painted *c.*1330, which are more extensive than in any other house in England. Scenes are taken from the Bible as well as popular folklore. The building is open to the public.

4. SOUTHWICK HALL
SOUTHWICK, Northamptonshire
13 miles south-west of Stamford

Part of the 14th-century house belonging to Sir John Knyvett, Lord Chancellor (d.1381), still survives. There is a 14th-century square tower in the south-west corner and a 14th-century door and spiral staircase in the great hall. The house is open to the public.

5. TRIANGULAR BRIDGE
CROWLAND, Lincolnshire
15 miles east of Stamford

Described by the antiquary Gough as 'the greatest curiosity in Britain, if not in Europe'. This unique late 14th-century bridge stands incongruously high and dry in the centre of Crowland. It formerly spanned branches of the Welland and Nene rivers. The large seated figure, probably of Christ, may have come from the gable of the abbey.

15TH CENTURY
PRIVATE WEALTH, PUBLIC SQUALOR
STAMFORD

1. ST JOHN'S CHURCH
St John's Street

St John's was completely rebuilt about 1450 by a wealthy syndicate of local merchants. Its tower is similar in style to the later one at St Martin's. The tightness of the site means the tower buttresses cascade onto the road. All the windows and doors have 4-centred arches which are typical of the period. Inside, the nave roof is embellished with angels holding musical instruments, books and other objects; angel roofs are more common in East Anglia (March, *Cambs.*). The beautiful wooden screens still survive but now divide the aisles from the eastern chapels. Some good 15th-century stained glass, including figures of saints, is scattered around the church.

117

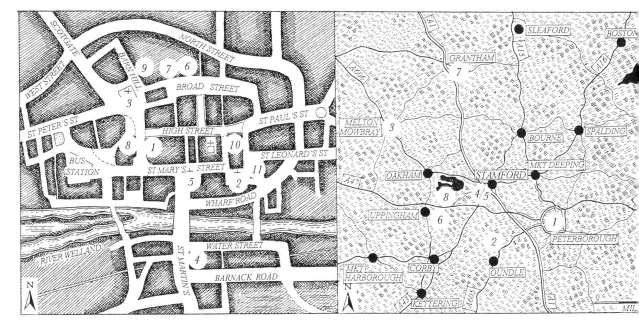

Above: *Buildings & sites from the 15th century*

2. ST GEORGE'S CHURCH
St George's Square

Much of the work here was funded by William de Bruges, the first Garter King of Arms, who bequeathed money in his will (1449) to rebuild the chancel. He also commissioned a series of stained glass windows depicting the Knights of the Garter. Unfortunately these were destroyed in 1736, but about 200 mottoes of founder members of the Garter are reset in a north nave window. The best stained glass, though, is in the south chancel window where there are two good mid 15th-century figures. *See also* C13*ST, 3*; C17*ST, 1*; C18*ST, 2*.

3. ALL SAINTS' CHURCH
All Saints' Place

The 13th-century church was substantially rebuilt in the late 15th century by the Browne family who were rich wool merchants. They certainly made their mark on the skyline of Stamford. The steeple, decorated with blind arcading and quatrefoils, is a fine companion for St Mary's; the slender pinnacle spire rises to 152ft. On the east face of the tower is a 15th-century clock face set into a window. Inside the church are various brasses of the Browne family. *See also ST, 6*; *ST, 7*; *ST, 8*; C13*ST, 2*; C16/17*SA, 8*.

4. ST MARTIN'S CHURCH
High Street St Martin's

Another complete 15th-century church. St Martin's was rebuilt around 1480 by Bishop Russell of Lincoln. Its sturdy tower is the echo of St John's across the river. The interior is very spacious with tall elegant arcades. The windows contain fragments of 15th-century stained glass taken from Tattershall (Lincs.) in the 1750s by the 9th Earl of Exeter. *See also* C16*ST, 1*; C18*ST, 1*.

5. ST MARY'S CHURCH
St Mary's Place

The main body of the church was rebuilt in the late 15th century. It has large windows and slender nave arcades. The north chapel was given a magnificent roof of golden bosses by William Hykeham and his wife just before 1484. Between the chapel and chancel is an impressive monument to Sir David Phillip (d. 1506) and his wife. *See also* C13*ST, 1*; C14*ST, 2*; C19*ST, 7*.

6. BROWNE'S HOSPITAL
Broad Street

One of the finest medieval almshouses in England. It was founded by William Browne, a wealthy wool merchant, in 1475-6 to provide accommodation for about 12 poor people. Although the design was traditional in having a

118

simple communal hall, it was unusual in having two first floor rooms. At the rear were a small cloister and service buildings. The main range survives despite alteration in 1870 by James Fowler of Louth (Lincs.). He removed the sleeping cubicles and rear service buildings and built separate accommodation around an extended cloister. He also added the small turret. The chapel has the best 15th-century stained glass in the town plus fine examples of Lincolnshire wooden screenwork. The hospital was used as the Old Infirmary and boardroom in the BBC's *Middlemarch* drama. The building is open to the public during the summer. *See also ST, 3*; *ST, 7*; *ST, 8*.

7. No. 3 BROAD STREET

Traditionally believed to be the site of the town house of the Browne family. A 15th-century crocketed gable survives at the rear of the Victorian east wing. *See also ST, 3*; *ST, 6*; *ST, 8*.

8. Nos. 6-7 RED LION SQUARE

Possibly the wool house of the Browne family. The building still retains many features of the medieval hall; the first floor is timber-framed and jettied. At the rear are the remains of a traceried 15th-century wooden window.
See also ST, 3 ST, 6; *ST, 7*

9. No. 16 BARN HILL

Former All Saints' Vicarage

A late 15th-century stone-built house; the small doorway has a 4-centred arch. The building may have originally had an open hall in the south half. Most of the windows are later and have Victorian artificial stone hoodmoulds.

10. Nos. 5-6 MAIDEN LANE

Behind the rebuilt 17th-century building is a reset 15th-century doorway. This came from a building demolished in 1966 at the east end of High Street. It has continuous mouldings and headstops.

11. Nos. 10-11 ST GEORGE'S STREET

Both houses probably originated as late-medieval open halls. No. 11 has an external chimney stack with an unusual circular top.

SURROUNDING AREA

1. PETERBOROUGH CATHEDRAL
PETERBOROUGH, Cambridgeshire
14 miles south-east of Stamford

The extravagant fan-vaulted retrochoir was built by Abbot Robert Kirkdon between *c.*1496 and 1508. It is similar in detail and quality to King's College Chapel in Cambridge and may have been designed by the same man, John Wastell. Also of this date is the Priory Gate. *See also C9SA, 3*; *C12SA, 1*; *C13SA, 1*.

2. ST MARY & ALL SAINTS' CHURCH
FOTHERINGHAY, Northamptonshire
12 miles south of Stamford

A stunning church; its huge octagonal bell tower is visible for miles around. The church was closely associated with the nearby castle which was rebuilt in the 14th century by Edmund Langley, son of Edward III and owner of Stamford; Richard III was born at the castle in 1452. In 1411, Edward of York founded a college at Fotheringhay and the church was completely rebuilt in the following 30 years. The church was originally twice its present size: the chancel, which was demolished in 1573, was as grand and ambitious as the tall, lofty nave. *See also C16SA, 12*.

3. ST MARY'S CHURCH
MELTON MOWBRAY
20 miles north-west of Stamford

Described by Pevsner as 'the stateliest and most impressive of all the churches in Leicestershire'. The church is 164 feet long with a tower 100 feet high. The most remarkable feature is the 15th-century clerestory which runs continuously over nave and transepts; it contains no fewer than 48 windows. The top stage of the tower, with its array of pinnacles, is of the same date.

4. ALL SAINTS' CHURCH
EASTON-ON-THE-HILL, Northamptonshire
2 miles south-west of Stamford
5. ST ANDREW'S CHURCH
COLLYWESTON, Northamptonshire
3 miles south-west of Stamford

Both churches have late 15th-century towers based on St John's in Stamford. The pinnacles are very pronounced. Also in Easton is a small late 15th-century stone-built priest's house now housing a museum of village bygones on the first floor. The building is open to the public.

6. LYDDINGTON BEDE HOUSE
LYDDINGTON, Rutland
14 miles south-west of Stamford
Originally a palace of the bishops of Lincoln. The existing building was part of a palace built by Bishop Alnwick (1436-49) and altered by Bishops Russell (1480-94; *see ST,* **4**) and Smith (1496-1514). After the Reformation the house went to the Crown and then to the Cecils of Burghley House; John Cecil converted it into an almshouse in 1602. It is an impressive 15th-century building characterised by big external chimney stacks and mullion and transom windows. The building is open to the public and the interior has many interesting features including an excellent arch- and wind-braced roof.

7. ANGEL AND ROYAL HOTEL
GRANTHAM, Lincolnshire
20 miles north-west of Stamford
One of the grandest pre-Reformation inns in England. The stone frontage dates from the late 15th century. It was here that Richard III signed the death warrant of the Duke of Buckingham.

8. WING TURF MAZE
WING, Rutland
10 miles south-west of Stamford
The maze is situated by the side of the road to Glaston. Its date and purpose are unknown but it is probably of late medieval origin. It is circular, 40ft in diameter and its design is identical to earlier mazes found on the floors of Saint-Quentin, Chartres and Poitiers Cathedrals in France. Similar turf mazes exist elsewhere in England but they are very rare.

16TH–17TH CENTURIES
MONASTERIES TO MANORS/RECESSION
STAMFORD

1. ST MARTIN'S CHURCH
High Street St Martin's
William Cecil's massive Renaissance tomb dominates the chancel of the church. The scale and quality of the monument (of *c.*1598) are comparable with those of tombs in Westminster Abbey. An effigy of Cecil in full regalia lies under an elegant canopy supported by 6 columns. It was possibly designed by Cornelius Cure, who is also credited with the monument in the Burghley Chapel to Richard Cecil (d.1552) and his wife. *See also SA,* **11**; *C15ST,* **4**; *C18ST,* **1**.

2. No. 40 ST MARY'S STREET
Recession meant that timber framing probably became more common in the town during the 16th century. This is one of the best examples. It has a timber-framed first floor with close-studded timbers.

3. Nos. 8-9 ST MARY'S HILL
A 16th-century jettied timber-framed range. The row originally continued up to St Mary's Passage but the northern part was demolished in 1886.

4. No. 19 ST MARY'S STREET
St Mary's Vaults
This building possibly originated as a late medieval inn. The first floor of the front range is timber-framed as is the tall gabled cross-wing. There is a carved head just above the carriageway.

5. Nos. 7-11 ST PAUL'S STREET
A delightful jumble of late medieval stone and timber-framed houses. The gabled cross-wings create a picturesque streetscape.

6. No. 20 HIGH STREET ST MARTIN'S
Many 16th- and 17th-century timber-framed buildings in Stamford are disguised behind later 18th-century facades. This 16th-century hall and cross-wing house has been stuccoed and gentrified.

SURROUNDING AREA
1. OAKHAM SCHOOL
OAKHAM, Rutland
10 miles west of Stamford
2. UPPINGHAM SCHOOL
UPPINGHAM, Rutland
15 miles south-west of Stamford
These late 16th-century school buildings, built by Robert Johnson from Stamford, can be found near the towns' churches. Both are stone-built single-room buildings with large mullion and transom windows.

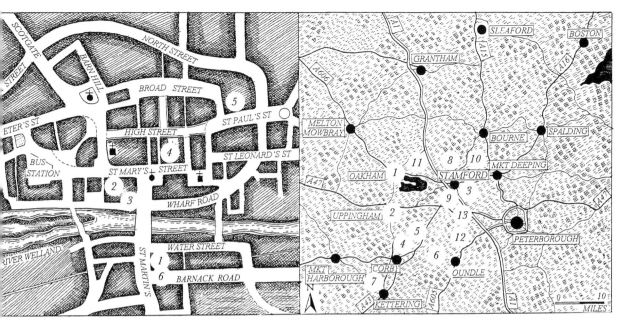

Above: Buildings & sites from the 16th/17th centuries

3. BURGHLEY HOUSE

1 mile south-east of Stamford

One of the grandest Elizabethan mansions in England. The house was built by William Cecil from the 1550s until 1587. The design of the house was influenced by Cecil's patron, the Duke of Somerset, whose Somerset House in London of *c*.1548-52 was the model for many great houses, including Longleat in Wiltshire. Burghley is based around a central courtyard with a massive medieval-style gate-house incorporated into the main west front. However, much of the detailing is Renaissance in feeling and reflects Cecil's architectural connections with the Continent. The highlight is the amazing roofline: towers, turrets, domes, balustrades, obelisks and tall Classical chimney stacks combine to create the illusion of an entire town. It can be compared with another Elizabethan 'prodigy' house at Kirby. The house is open to the public. *See also SA, 9; C17SA, 15; C18SA, 5.*

4. KIRBY HALL

Near DEENE, Northamptonshire
17 miles south-west of Stamford

This huge, compelling ruin is one of England's best Elizabethan houses. It is quadrangular, like Burghley, but the architectural detail is unique:

giant pilaster strips, common in France but virtually unheard of in England, articulate the courtyard facades. The house was begun in 1570 by Sir Humphrey Stafford and was continued in the 1580s by one of Elizabeth I's prodigies, Sir Christopher Hatton, who lived at Holdenby (Northants.). Two top-quality bays, attributed to Inigo Jones, were added in the early 17th century. Despite its ostentation, Kirby has been neglected for many centuries. It is now open to the public.

5. DEENE PARK

DEENE, Northamptonshire
15 miles south-west of Stamford

Another great Elizabethan mansion only 2 miles from the incredible Kirby. The house was built from *c*.1520 to 1585 by the Brudenell family who still live there. Like Burghley and Kirby, it is arranged around a central courtyard, but it has less of their architectural virtuosity. The house is open to the public.

6. LYVEDEN NEW BIELD

LYVEDEN, Northamptonshire
20 miles south-west of Stamford

A large summer house built by Sir Thomas Tresham of Rushton from 1594 until his death in 1605. Like the *SA, 7* the building is symbolic: it is in the shape of a Greek cross alluding to Christ's

121

Passion. The building was never finished and it now stands isolated in rolling Northamptonshire countryside. It is open to the public.

7. TRIANGULAR LODGE
RUSHTON, Northamptonshire
25 miles south-west of Stamford

One of the most bizarre follies in England. The lodge was built by Sir Thomas Tresham between 1594 and 1597. Everything about the building is based on the number 3; this is a conceit based on Tresham's name (their emblem was a trefoil) and religion (they were Catholics, so the building symbolises the Trinity). Pevsner calls it 'the most perfect example in architectural terms of the Elizabethan love of the conceit'. The lodge is open to the public. *See also SA, 6.*

8. TOLETHORPE HALL
TOLETHORPE, Rutland
2 miles north of Stamford

The medieval house was rebuilt in the late 16th and early 17th centuries by the Browne family; the hall was the birthplace of Robert Browne, founder of the religious group, the Brownists. The main south front retains unusual cross-wings parallel to the main range, but there have been many 18th- and 19th-century alterations. The house is now the home of the Stamford Shakespeare Company.

9. WOTHORPE HOUSE
WOTHORPE, Cambridgeshire
1 mile south-west of Stamford

Wothorpe was built by Thomas Cecil in the early 17th century as a dower house for widows of the family (Burghley had previously fulfilled this function). The strange ruins of the tower house survive; the four corner turrets originally had ogee domes as at Burghley. But, unlike Burghley and Robert Cecil's Hatfield House, the window detailing here was influenced by Italian Mannerism. In front of the house was a forecourt flanked by wings; a large 17th-century barn still stands. The house became derelict during the 18th century and was plundered for stone. It has been used for locations in BBC's *Dr Who*. It can be reached by local footpaths. *See also SA, 3.*

10. CASEWICK HALL
CASEWICK, Uffington, Lincolnshire
3 miles north-east of Stamford

The present hall was begun in 1621 by William

Trollope of Thurlby. The south range of his building still survives. A good view can be obtained via public footpaths. *See also C18SA, 4.*

11. EXTON OLD HALL
EXTON, Rutland
8 miles north-west of Stamford

The ruins of the early 17th-century house of the Harrington and later Noel family can be seen from the road to the church. The house was burnt out in 1810 but most of the walls of the great hall survive. In the church are outstanding monuments to Robert Kelway, lawyer, who died in 1580, and Sir James Harrington and his wife, who both died in 1591. Compare with Cecil's tomb *ST, 1.*

12. FOTHERINGHAY CASTLE
FOTHERINGHAY, Northamptonshire
12 miles south of Stamford

The site is chiefly remembered as the place where Mary Queen of Scots was executed on 8 February 1587, following a year's imprisonment there. It is accessible via a farm track. *See also C15SA, 2.*

13. WANSFORD BRIDGE
WANSFORD, Cambridgeshire
6 miles south of Stamford

This superb bridge carries the old Great North Road over the River Nene. The seven northern arches of the bridge are dated 1577 and give a good impression of a typical medieval bridge. Like the old bridge at Stamford, the carriageway is only one lane wide.

17TH CENTURY
RECESSION/CIVIL WAR/ ROADS TO PROSPERITY
STAMFORD

1. ST GEORGE'S CHURCH
St George's Square

St George's is unusual in having a late 17th-century west tower. It is rectangular in section and has a slightly military appearance with plain stonework and pronounced battlements. *See also* C13ST, *3*; C15ST, *2*; C18ST, *2.*

2. LORD BURGHLEY'S HOSPITAL
Station Road

An almshouse founded by William Cecil in 1597. The eastern ranges are the earliest, but the main visual impression is created by the later 17th-

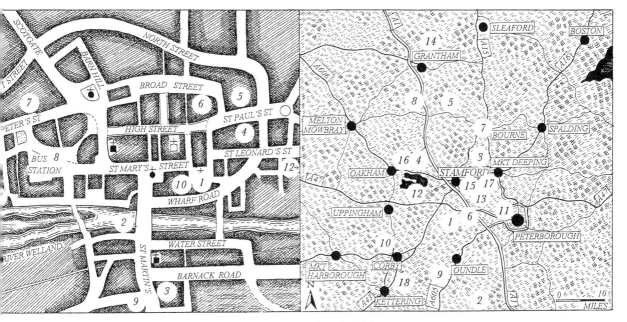

Above: *Buildings & sites from the 17th century*

century range along Station Road, altered 1964. Unlike Browne's Hospital (C15*ST*, **6**), the accommodation is in separate collegiate-style units. The tall chimney stacks along the river front are 18th-century.

3. BULL AND SWAN
No. 25 High Street St Martin's
The medieval hall was given a fashionable stone front of gabled canted bays in the early-mid 17th century. The 1st floor windows are unique in Stamford in this period in that they have transoms. Like *ST*, **6**, the bay over the carriageway is timber-framed.

4. No. 32 ST PAUL'S STREET
Perhaps the earliest of the new, large stone-built 17th-century houses. The doorway has a 4-centred arch which suggests an early 17th-century date. The canted bays have no gables.

5. No. 12 ST PAUL'S STREET
A fine mature 'vernacular' style frontage with canted and gabled bays. It was added to the medieval building in 1663 by the Norris family who were prosperous bell founders. It has the same form as *ST*, **6** but suffers from the later insertion of sash windows.

6. No. 32 BROAD STREET
The finest 'vernacular' style 17th-century house in Stamford and one of the most attractive houses in the town. An elegant, symmetrical composition with 2 canted gabled bays and a central doorway. Windows are metal-framed and leaded. Although the main range is stone-built, there is a cheaper timber-framed bay over the carriage entrance. The house was probably built after the Restoration.

7. Nos. 13-15 ALL SAINTS' STREET
8. BUS STATION WAITING ROOM
Sheepmarket
Nos. 13-15 form a group of mid-late 17th-century 'vernacular' buildings. No 13 has a late 17th-century square-sided bay embellished with quoins, while No. 14 has the more usual gabled and canted bay. A combination of square and canted bays can be found in the bus station building in Sheepmarket. This altered facade, dated 1661, was moved to here in 1936 from the back of No. 61 High Street.

9. Nos 39-40 HIGH STREET
ST MARTIN'S
A fine row of 3 canted 17th-century bays positioned right at the southern extremity of the town. The bays were raised by an extra storey in

the early 18th century.

10. No. 19 ST GEORGE'S SQUARE

Dated 1674, this is the first Classically-inspired house in Stamford. It was influenced by Thorpe Hall near Peterborough (*SA*, *11*) and was designed by John Sturges, the architect of Lyndon Hall (*SA*, *12*). It was built for Daniel Wigmore, a wealthy woollen draper. The house has two rows of dormer windows, a feature usually found in Belgium and Holland. It is the chimney stacks, though, which are the highlight. These are in the Artisan Mannerist style, which is a provincial interpretation of early 17th-century Italian design. A similar stack can be found between Nos. 2 and 3 Broad Street.

11. KING'S MILL

Bath Row

There has been a mill on this site since before Domesday (1086). The present water mill was built by the Cecil family around 1640 for grinding corn. It is a marvellous example of early industrial architecture. The mill and tail races still survive.

12. HUDD'S MILL
& WELLAND NAVIGATION CANAL

Uffington Meadows
¾ mile east of town centre

Another 17th-century water-powered mill, here situated by the weir east of the town. It was from near Hudd's Mill that the Welland Navigation Canal began. The canal was opened in 1664 and ran for 9 miles to Market Deeping; it was one of the first industrial canals in England. It fell into disuse following the arrival of the railway in the mid 19th century. The banks of the canal can be followed along public footpaths to Uffington. A lock survives at Market Deeping.

SURROUNDING AREA

1. ST LEONARD'S CHURCH

APETHORPE, Northamptonshire
10 miles south-west of Stamford

The colossal marble monument to Sir Anthony Mildmay of Apethorpe House dates from *c*.1617 and is one of the finest early 17th-century memorials in England. It is topped by a huge canopy which almost touches the ceiling of the contemporary chapel. The chapel is adorned with beautiful enamel painted glass.

2. ST MARY'S CHURCH

LEIGHTON BROMSWOLD, Cambridgeshire
25 miles south of Stamford

The church has an outstanding interior created by the poet George Herbert (1593-1633) who was appointed to the Prebend here in 1626. The testered pulpit and reader's desk dominate, emphasising the equal importance of preaching and prayer. After Herbert's death, his poems were published by Nicholas Ferrar, leader of the community at nearby Little Gidding.

3. ST MARTIN'S CHURCH

BARHOLM, Lincolnshire
5 miles east of Stamford

The tower was rebuilt in 1648 during the Civil War and has a revealing inscription: 'Was ever such a thing since the creation. A new steeple built in the time of vexation'.

4. ST PETER & ST PAUL'S CHURCH

EXTON, Rutland
8 miles north-west of Stamford

The north aisle of the church is dominated by the vast Baroque monument to the 3rd Viscount Camden designed by Grinling Gibbons and erected in 1686 at a cost of £1,000. It is one of the most outstanding church monuments in the country. Camden fought for the Royalists during the Civil War and was captured by Cromwell at the siege of Burghley House. *See also* C16*SA*, *11*.

5. GRAMMAR SCHOOL

CORBY GLEN, Lincolnshire
15 miles north of Stamford

A rare survival of a small 17th-century village school. It was built by the Berties of Grimsthorpe in 1673. The tall pedimented porch with its oval window was added in 1691. The building is now a memorial library and art gallery.

6. HAYCOCK INN

WANSFORD, Cambridgeshire
6 miles south of Stamford

Wansford was on the Old Great North Road and its wide main street is a witness to the coaching era. The Haycock is a great late 17th-century coaching inn, comparable with the George in Stamford (*see* C18*ST*, *3*).

7. RED HALL

BOURNE, Lincolnshire
10 miles north-east of Stamford

A grand early 17th-century town mansion possibly designed by John Thorpe, a surveyor in the Office of Works. The house can be visited by arrangement.

8. WOOLSTHORPE MANOR

WOOLSTHORPE, Lincolnshire
11 miles north of Stamford

An excellent example of a small, unpretentious 17th-century manor house. It was built around 1620 and has a typical T-shaped floor plan. The interior is beautifully preserved. The house is famous as being the birthplace of Sir Isaac Newton (b. 1642). It is open to the public.

9. LILFORD HALL

Lilford Park, near OUNDLE, Northamptonshire
18 miles south of Stamford

The grounds have been converted into a country park. The house, however, has fine elevations dating from *c.*1635 and 1656. It is open to the public.

10. ROCKINGHAM CASTLE

ROCKINGHAM, Northamptonshire
18 miles south-west of Stamford

The castle was substantially rebuilt in the mid-late 17th century following severe damage in the Civil War. The castle was used in the filming of the Civil War television series *By the Sword Divided. See also C12SA,* **8.**

11. THORPE HALL

LONGTHORPE, Peterborough, Cambridgeshire
13 miles south-east of Stamford

An important house in the early development of Classical architecture in England. The house was built in 1653-56 by Peter Mills for Chief Justice St John. It has elegant symmetrical facades. Peterborough also has the Guildhall in Cathedral Square. The hall, built in 1671, is supported on a fine arcade of Tuscan columns. See also *SA,* **12.**

12. LYNDON HALL

LYNDON, Rutland
8 miles south-west of Stamford

Lyndon Hall was probably influenced by Thorpe Hall (above): it is square, of 2 storeys of 7 bays with a hipped roof topped with 4 chimney stacks. It was built between 1671 and 1677 and was designed by John Sturges in collaboration with the owner, Sir Abel Barker. *See also ST,* **10.**

13. WALCOT HALL

Near BARNACK, Cambridgeshire
4 miles south-east of Stamford

An excellent Restoration house built in 1678 by Sir Hugh Chomley, 4th Baron of Whitby, and designed by John Webb. It soon passed into the Noel and then the Neville families. The house was used as Freshitt Hall, home of the Chettams, in BBC's *Middlemarch.* The gardens are occasionally open to the public.

14. BELTON HOUSE

BELTON, near Grantham, Lincolnshire
22 miles north of Stamford

Pevsner says 'Belton is perhaps the most satisfying among the later 17th century houses in England.' It was begun in 1685 by Sir John Brownlow and was possibly designed by William Winde. The design was based on Clarendon House in Piccadilly, London, of 1664; it has an H-shaped floor plan, large sash windows, hipped roofs with dormers and a cupola. The interior has finely carved 17th-century wooden panels by, or in the style of, Grinling Gibbons. The house is open to the public.

15. BURGHLEY HOUSE

1 mile south-east of Stamford

In the 1680s and 1690s, John Cecil, 5th Earl of Exeter, transformed the Elizabethan interior into a Baroque showcase, inspired perhaps by his brother-in-law's work at Chatsworth. A series of State Rooms were created, culminating in the Heaven Room and Hell Room. These featured extravagant painted walls and ceilings by Antonio Verrio. (Verrio also worked for Charles Bertie at *SA,* **17.**) The cost virtually bankrupted the Cecil estate. *See also C16SA,* **3;** C18SA, **5.**

16. BURLEY HOUSE

BURLEY-ON-THE-HILL, Rutland
9 miles west of Stamford

The house is spectacularly sited on a wooded hill now overlooking Rutland Water. The original house, built by the 1st Duke of Buckingham, was destroyed in the Civil War. It was rebuilt in grand style by Daniel Finch, 2nd Earl of Nottingham between 1696 and 1700. The north front of the house is preceded by a huge 'piazza' framed by colonnades reminiscent of St Peter's in Rome. Pevsner describes it as 'the most sweeping composition of its date in England'. The house itself copies earlier buildings such as Ragley, Warwickshire.

17. UFFINGTON HOUSE
UFFINGTON, Lincolnshire
2 miles east of Stamford

The Restoration house built by Charles Bertie in *c.*1681 burnt down in 1904; the interior was painted by Verrio (*see SA*, *15*). However, the magnificent gate-piers of *c.*1700 still survive. Pevsner rates them as the best in the county. They might have been designed by John Lumley, who probably did the identical ones at *SA*, *16*. The Coade Stone urns are 19th-century.

18. BOUGHTON HOUSE
Near KETTERING, Northamptonshire
22 miles south-west of Stamford

The great north front of Boughton is possibly the most French-looking 17th-century building in England. It was built by the 1st Duke of Montagu between 1690 and 1709; the French influence must be the result of the Duke's appointment as Ambassador to Paris during the 1670s. Some of the avenues of the French-style formal grounds survive. The house is open to the public.

18TH CENTURY
ROADS TO PROSPERITY
STAMFORD

1. ST MARTIN'S CHURCH
High Street St Martin's

The colossal Baroque memorial to John, 5th Earl of Exeter, was designed in Rome by Pierre-Étienne Monnot and was erected by William Palmer in 1704. Monnot did the tomb of Pope Innocent XI in St Peter's in Rome. Marble effigies recline on a large sarcophagus while figures of Victory and Art look on. Behind is a tall flattened pyramid. It is comparable in quality with C17*SA*, *4*. See also C15*ST*, *4*; C16*ST*, *1*.

2. ST GEORGE'S CHURCH
St George's Square

In the chancel is an accomplished monument to Richard Cust, designed in 1797 by John Bacon. A life-size allegorical female figure stands by a pedestal topped with a bust. The Custs lived at Blackfriars House off the south side of Wharf Road. See also C13*ST*, *3*; C15*ST*, *2*; C17*ST*, *1*.

3. GEORGE HOTEL
High Street St Martin's

The street front of the hotel was rebuilt by the Cecils in 1724. The plain 3-storey 5-bay elevation was designed by George Portwood and includes the Cecil coat of arms in the parapet. The famous 'gallows' inn sign was possibly a later addition to help prevent the front wall from bulging. The rear ranges are late 18th-century. See also C17*SA*, *6*.

4. ASSEMBLY ROOMS
St George's Square

Assembly Rooms were entertainment and social centres for dancing, balls and card playing. Stamford's Assembly Rooms was one of the earliest in the country, being built by the Cecils and dancing master Askew Kirk in 1727. A severe Palladian exterior conceals a large hall which retains fine original features including a 17th-century style chimney piece and scrolled door frames. The building is now part of Stamford Arts Centre.

5. STAMFORD THEATRE
St Mary's Street

The theatre has had a chequered history. It was built in 1768 but was forced to close in 1871; happily, it was refurbished and reopened in 1978 as part of Stamford Arts Centre. The building is a superb example of a small, provincial Georgian theatre. The theatre was used as Bulstrode's Bank in BBC's *Middlemarch*.

6. HOPKINS' HOSPITAL
St Peter's Street

An almshouse for poor married couples built in 1770 by John Hopkins, the mayor. It heralds the arrival of the Gothick style to Stamford. However, although the windows and doors have pointed arches, the composition is still symmetrical. The parapet is battlemented in imitation of the nearby town walls.

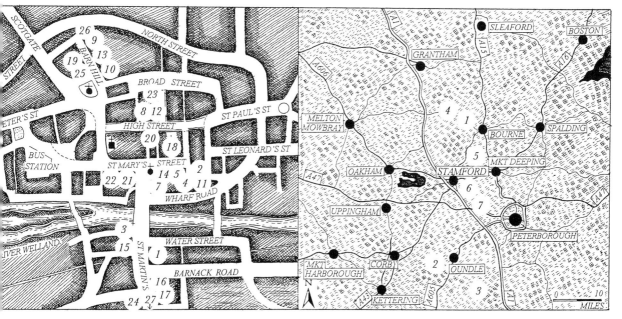

Above: Buildings & sites from the 18th century

7. TOWN HALL
St Mary's Hill/ St Mary's Place

Partially funded by the Cecils of Burghley, this building replaced the 16th-century Town Hall which stood at the north end of the Town Bridge. It was built in 1775-6 and was possibly designed by Henry Tatam, a local cabinet maker. The detailing is very flat and effete and can be compared with Tatam's own house, *see ST, 26*. Both elevations of the Town Hall are the same with a projecting central section of 3 bays focused on the Borough arms.

8. Nos. 14-17 HIGH STREET

This huge 3-storey, 12-bay terrace must have been one of the largest secular buildings in the town when it was put up in *c*.1700. It shares stylistic similarities with No. 19 St George's Square (C17*ST, 10*), most notably the bolection window mouldings which here continue from bay to bay. The whole range is rendered.

9. No. 12 BARN HILL

A town house of *c*.1700 based on the new ideas of Classical proportion. It has 5 regular bays and 5 corresponding dormer windows. The curved porch hood is supported by splendid carved brackets.

10. No. 3 ALL SAINTS' PLACE

One of the finest Georgian houses in the town. Built in 1716, the house is a perfect essay in proportion and restraint. It has 5 bays with plain moulded windows. The rusticated doorway is in the style invented by James Gibbs (1682-1754) and popularised in pattern books by Batty Langley and other writers. It was the home of the Lydgates in BBC's *Middlemarch*. Compare with Brazenose House of 1723 on St Paul's Street.

11. No. 20 ST GEORGE'S SQUARE

A very severe early 18th-century town house. The windows have no mouldings and the pilastered and pedimented doorway is mannered and restrained. This plain style became popular again in Stamford later in the century. For another early 18th-century example see Nos. 47-50 High Street St Martin's.

12. No. 59 & No. 21 HIGH STREET

No. 59 is early 18th-century, tall and narrow with a wonderful bracketed cornice. No. 21, at the corner with Ironmonger Street, is slightly later (1732) with heavy rusticated windows divided by giant fluted pilasters. It heralds the beginning of a more jazzy, ornamental phase of building.

13. No. 13 BARN HILL

A superb 18th-century town house, perhaps the best in the town. It can be dated to 1740 by the rainwater heads. The window and door detailing is of the highest quality: the ground floor windows have Gibbsian surrounds with keystoned heads, while the upper windows have lugged surrounds with triangular pediments. The dormers have alternating triangular and segmental tops. The doorway is wide and rather severe. The design is identical to the garden front of Leasingham Manor, just north of Sleaford.

14. Nos. 2-3 ST MARY'S PLACE

No. 2 is a grand town house dating from the 2nd quarter of the 18th century. The left hand bay is left plain outside the main composition which is framed by giant rusticated pilasters, possibly inspired by Vanbrugh's Grimsthorpe (*SA, 3*). The upper windows have Gibbsian surrounds similar to those at *ST, 15*. No. 3 is a slightly later extension; it is punctuated by superimposed Doric pilasters.

15. Nos. 66-67 HIGH STREET
ST MARTIN'S

An excellent pair of unaltered Georgian houses dating from *c.*1740. Many of the features have been copied from contemporary pattern books. The giant rusticated pilasters and Gibbsian ground floor windows can also be found at *ST, 14*. The fanlights over the doors retain their original glass.

16. No. 33 HIGH STREET ST MARTIN'S

This early-mid 18th-century house is notable for its use of superimposed pilasters (*see also ST, 14*). Here the orders are Ionic and Corinthian.

17. No. 35 HIGH STREET ST MARTIN'S

A classic pattern book house brimming with Gibbsian rustication. It probably dates from *c.*1740 and is the logical conclusion of the pattern book style in Stamford. After this, houses in the town gradually became plainer.

18. Nos. 22-24 ST MARY'S STREET

A superb group of Georgian houses justly featured in BBC's *Middlemarch* drama. No. 22 dates from *c.*1740 and is a continuation of the simpler, more sober school of design first seen at *SA, 10*; it even has an identical Gibbsian doorway. No. 23 is

much tighter in its proportions but the result is exemplary. The lugged first floor windows are copied from next door, but there is also a fine moulded cornice and a beautiful doorway with fluted Ionic pilasters. No. 24 was built shortly afterwards as an office for the owner of No. 23; it is the earliest known office building in Stamford. As in other 18th-century houses, the doorway has been moved from the centre to create a larger room inside; see also No. 18 St George's Square.

19. BARN HILL HOUSE
Barn Hill

Stamford's largest town house is an amalgamation of three building periods: 1698, when it was first built; mid 18th century when it was refronted, and 1843-4 when it was dressed up for receiving government ministers during Queen Victoria's visit to Burghley House. The dominant impression, however, is of mid 18th-century grandeur. The house was used as the New Fever Hospital in BBC's *Middlemarch*.

20. Nos. 54-55 HIGH STREET

A stone-built mid 18th-century facade provides a fashionable frontage to a 16th-century timber-framed building. It is an elegant composition with moulded window frames, rusticated quoins and a parapet. *See also C16ST, 6*.

21. Nos. 1-2; Nos. 11-12; Nos. 14-16
ST MARY'S HILL
22. Nos. 34-39 ST MARY'S STREET
23. Nos. 12-14 IRONMONGER STREET

These buildings are part of the 9th Earl of Exeter's grand rebuilding programme. The scheme fortunately stopped at his death in 1793, for had it continued it might have threatened the architectural variety of the town. The buildings are mainly plain, unadorned terraces of 3 storeys built of rubble stone. Their detrimental impact can be felt along St Mary's Street. The architect of some of the work was Thomas Lumby of Lincoln.

24. No. 42; No. 43
HIGH STREET ST MARTIN'S

These two houses epitomise the late 18th-century move towards simplicity. Both date from *c.*1790 and both reject superfluous ornament. No. 43 is a wide, stretched composition centred on a single moulded window frame and doorway. No. 42 has a pilastered and pedimented doorway. Compare these houses with the exuberance of No. 35 opposite (*ST*, *17*).

25. No. 16 ALL SAINTS' PLACE

A tall 3-storey town house of 1793. The bowed window bays must have been very fashionable; they are the earliest of their kind in Stamford. The bow window was to become very popular in the Regency period together with the Mansard roof, also seen here.

26. STUKELEY HOUSE
Barn Hill

William Stukeley, the famous 18th-century antiquarian, lived in a house on this site during the 1730s and 1740s. While living here he wrote his pioneering books on the Stonehenge and Avebury stone circles. It was Stukeley who began the erroneous rumour that Charles I spent his last night of freedom in this house. The present house was built by Henry Tatam in *c*.1800; *see ST*, *7*.

27. BOTTLE LODGES
Old Great North Road

Just beyond High Street St Martin's are the gate lodges of Burghley House built in 1801. This elaborate conceit on Elizabethan architecture was designed by local architect William Legg for the 1st Marquess of Exeter. The style is influenced by both Burghley and Wothorpe. The cost was about £9,000! *See also* C16*SA*, *3*; C16/17*SA*, *9*.

SURROUNDING AREA

1. ST MICHAEL'S CHURCH
EDENHAM, Lincolnshire
10 miles north-east of Stamford

The church contains the monuments of the Bertie and Willoughby families, Earls of Lindsey and Dukes of Ancaster (*see SA*, *3*). It is the largest series in any church in Lincolnshire. The collection of 18th-century memorials is particularly impressive. It includes work by Henry Cheere (1728; 1741); Henry and Peter Scheermakers (1728; 1738) and Charles Harris of London (1778/9).

2. ST RUMBOLD'S CHURCH
STOKE DOYLE, Northamptonshire
16 miles south of Stamford

There are few complete 18th-century churches around Stamford; this is perhaps the best. The church was built between 1722-25 and stands

aloof in the fields away from the village. It has a fine tower and a Venetian east window. It retains its original benches and pulpit.

3. ST JOHN'S CHURCH
LITTLE GIDDING, Cambridgeshire
16 miles south of Stamford

A diminutive church serving an isolated Puritan community. The original brick building was erected by Nicholas Ferrar in the early 17th century (*see* C17*SA*, *2*) but it was rebuilt in 1714 when a severe Classical stone front was added. T. S. Eliot wrote a poem about the Little Gidding community in the last of the *Four Quartets*.

4. GRIMSTHORPE CASTLE
GRIMSTHORPE, Lincolnshire
10 miles north of Stamford

Grimsthorpe is the most important 18th-century house in the area. The north front was rebuilt for the 1st Duke of Ancaster by Sir John Vanbrugh (of Blenheim fame) from 1722 up to Vanbrugh's death in 1726; it was probably completed by Nicholas Hawksmoor. This is Vanburgh's last work and is based on Seaton Delaval in Northumbria (*c*.1720) and Lumley Castle in County Durham (*c*.1722). The central block is flanked by pairs of giant rusticated Doric columns topped with groups of sculpture; all very Baroque. Pevsner says it is 'the most magnificent exposition of the theme in England'. The house was used as Quallingham, home of Tertius Lydgate's uncle, in BBC's *Middlemarch*. The house is open to the public. *See also SA*, *1*; C13*SA*, *9*.

5. CASEWICK HALL
Near UFFINGTON, Lincolnshire
3 miles east of Stamford

Pevsner says 'few houses in the county fill one with such delight'. The main west front was rebuilt for Sir William Trollope in the Gothick style in 1786-9 by William Legg of Stamford. The composition is centred on a Rococo-Gothick centre-piece with ogee windows. The whole 15-bay front is topped with battlemented and pinnacled gables. The house can be seen from a public footpath. *See also* C16/17*SA*, *10*.

6. BURGHLEY PARK
½ mile south-west of Stamford

The park was redesigned in the picturesque style by the famous 18th-century landscape designer,

Capability Brown. He worked at Burghley from 1756 to 1779. He designed the Lion Bridge over the new lake and the Gothick style Orangery, now used as a tea room. *See also* C16*SA*, *3*.

7. SACREWELL WATER MILL
Near Wansford, Cambridgeshire
6 miles south of Stamford

An 18th-century water mill complete with original machinery. The mill and farm museum are open to the public.

19TH CENTURY
ROTTEN BOROUGH/ TOWARDS EQUALITY
STAMFORD

1. METHODIST CHAPEL
Barn Hill

Just visible between the later chapel and No. 10 Barn Hill. The chapel was built in 1803 and altered in 1863. Around the central Venetian window are sculpted panels of Faith, Hope and Charity. *See also ST*, *6*.

2. CONGREGATIONAL CHAPEL
Star Lane

A large red brick preaching box built in 1819. It has a shallow hipped roof typical of the period. The galleried interior still survives.

3. BAPTIST CHAPEL
North Street

Originally built in 1834. Little survives of the original building which was altered and refronted in a coarse Italianate style in 1900 by local architect Joseph Boothroyd Corby.

4. ST MICHAEL'S CHURCH
High Street

Sadly mutilated during conversion to shops and offices in 1982; Pevsner calls it 'an unsympathetic use and an appalling conversion'. The church was built following the collapse of the medieval church during alterations in 1832. The new St Michael's was designed by John Brown of Norwich and is an early example of the academic Gothic Revival; its detailing is based on the Lady Chapel of Salisbury Cathedral. The *Stamford Mercury* described it on completion in 1836 as 'one of the most beautiful buildings in the kingdom'. The interior, however, was more like an 18th-century preaching box, with galleries and a tiny chancel.

5. OUR LADY AND ST AUGUSTINE'S ROMAN CATHOLIC CHURCH
Broad Street

A combined church, manse (vicarage) and school room. The ensemble was designed by Roman Catholic architect George Goldie in 1862-4. The style is robust 13th-century Gothic presided over by a crazy Continental-style bell turret.

6. METHODIST CHAPEL
Barn Hill

The new Methodist Chapel was built in 1886 to designs by local architect J. T. Ward. It is an uninspiring neo-Gothic preaching box. *See also ST*, *1*.

7. ST MARY'S CHURCH
St Mary's Place

The chancel was given an important Arts and Crafts restoration in 1890-91, supervised by John Dando Sedding. It includes a spectacular painted ceiling and a bronze altar frontal by Stirling Lee. *See also* C13*ST*, *1*; C14*ST*, *2*; C15*ST*, *5*.

8. SHAMBLES PORTICO/ PUBLIC LIBRARY
High Street

Formerly an open portico into the shambles or butchers' market. It was designed by William Legg and opened in 1808. The design was based on Inigo Jones' St Paul's Church in Covent Garden, London. It was infilled and converted into a library and museum in 1906.

9. STAMFORD HOTEL
St Mary's Street

One of the grandest Regency hotels in the country. It was designed by John Linnell Bond of London for Sir Gerard Noel of Exton Hall. Its ambitious grandeur was the result of its intended role as a centre of political opposition to the Tory Cecils. Building work began in 1810, but the lavish scale, with giant Corinthian columns and statue of Justice by John Rossi, was excessive for the restricted site (Noel actually tried to secure the demolition of St Mary's Church). Work was suspended following Noel's election defeat and a disastrous fire at Exton Hall forced him to sell the hotel; incidentally, the new Exton Hall, begun in 1811, is also the work of Bond. The hotel finally opened around 1816. It is now Stamford Walk shopping centre.

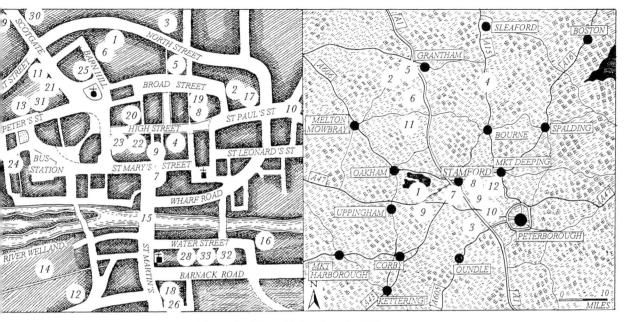

Above: *Buildings & sites from the 19th century*

10. STAMFORD AND RUTLAND INFIRMARY
Uffington Road

The Infirmary was built in 1826 and was designed to look like a country home. The design, by J. P. Gandy, heralded the arrival of the revived Tudor-Gothic style to Stamford. The style was to dominate 19th-century architecture in the town.

11. TRUESDALE'S HOSPITAL
Scotgate

12. FRYER'S CALLIS
Kettering Road

Two Tudor-Gothic almshouses designed by George Basevi in 1832-3. Basevi was a pupil of Sir John Soane and architect of the Neo-Classical Fitzwilliam Museum in Cambridge. Truesdale's Hospital is the more ambitious and bears the quartered arms of Thomas Truesdale.

13. STAMFORD INSTITUTION
St Peter's Hill

An amazing Greek/Egyptian-style building designed in 1842 by one of Stamford's most inventive architects, Bryan Browning. The tapering tomb-like doorway is the highlight. It was built as an education and social centre and incorporated a museum, library, lecture room and laboratory. On the roof was a camera obscura

which was demolished in 1910. *See also SA, 4.*

14. MIDLAND RAILWAY STATION
Off Station Road

One of the most picturesque railway stations in the country. A delightful asymmetric Tudor Gothic design by Sancton Wood of 1848. The weather vane on the turret has the initials of the Syston to Peterborough line. The cast iron bridge is a standard Midland Railway design of 1889.

15. TOWN BRIDGE & TOLL HOUSE

The Town Bridge was rebuilt with the arrival of the railway, but a series of mishaps meant it was not completed until 1849. It was designed by local architect Edward Browning, who also built the early 17th-century style Toll House. Nos. 3 and 4 St Mary's Hill and the end wall of Lord Burghley's Hospital were also altered to make them stylistically compatible.

16. STAMFORD EAST STATION
Water Street

This building looks more like an Elizabethan manor house than a railway station. Stamford East opened in 1856 and was the terminus of 2 branch lines, one to Essendine and the other to Wansford. The station was designed by William Hurst and was funded by the Cecil family of

Burghley House.

17. STAMFORD SCHOOL
St Paul's Street
18. HIGH SCHOOL
High Street St Martin's
Stamford School was greatly extended in 1874 as part of a unified schools scheme. The new buildings were designed by Hay and Oliver of London in a free-Gothic style. The High School for girls opened 3 years later. It was designed by Edward Browning in a contemporary adaptation of 15th-century Gothic.

19. TECHNICAL INSTRUCTION SCHOOL
Stamford Museum, Broad Street
A self-conscious building intended to harmonise with the Georgian architecture of the street. It was designed by local architect J. C. Traylen and was opened in 1894. It is now Stamford Museum.

20. GOTHIC HOUSE
No. 10 High Street
A romantic Victorian confection of 1849. The pastiche timber-framing and exuberant barge boards would be more at home in the West Midlands. It was the town post office from the early 19th century to 1866.

21. THE SCOTGATE
No. 5 Scotgate
A pub built in 1871 entirely out of terracotta manufactured at John Marriot Blashfield's Wharf Road factory. The Italianate facade features Hermes and Bacchus while up above is a craggy terracotta re-creation of the Phipps Brewery trade mark. For another Blashfield building see No. 30 High Street.

22. No. 58 HIGH STREET
Built in 1871-2, this is one of the most accomplished Victorian buildings in the town. It has a flat Gothic facade animated by superb polychromatic detailing executed in different coloured stones and tiles.

23. LLOYD'S BANK
No. 65 High Street
An Italianate Renaissance 'palazzo' style building built in Portland and Bath stone by a non-local architect, William Talbot-Brown of Welling-

borough (Northants.). It was built in 1880 for the Northamptonshire Banking Company. Rail travel meant it was feasible to import stone for imposing corporate projects.

24. AUSTIN HOUSE
Austin Street (view from Bath Row)
The street front is a bleak stone wall with a central bow window. The garden facade, however, has elegant bows with Venetian windows; it is described by Pevsner as 'the prettiest in Stamford'. Built in *c*.1800 this is undoubtedly the best Regency house in the town.

25. No. 3 BARN HILL
A pretty Regency house with a single bowed window bay and delicate Chinese style fretwork porch.

26. No. 30 HIGH STREET ST MARTIN'S
The ground floor has all the hallmarks of the Regency period: an ornate cast iron balcony is supported by a Doric porch, a bay window with charming Gothick tracery, and to the right, a single Doric column. The house was built *c*.1820.

27. RUTLAND TERRACE
Tinwell Road
A high-class speculative housing project built on the site of the bowling green, 1829-31. It is an elegant Regency terrace divided by giant anthemion-topped pilasters and centred on a large house with a decorative cast iron balcony. The earliest houses were stuccoed.

28. LUMBY'S TERRACE
Off Water Street
The best early industrial housing in the town, built by Moses Lumby, a butcher, around 1840. They were probably maltsters' dwellings. Like many of the early courts and slums, the buildings were at right angles to the street, but only the west terrace now survives. The houses have horizontal-sliding sash windows (called Yorkshire sash windows).

29. ROCK TERRACE
30. ROCK HOUSE
Scotgate
An ambitious building project erected 1841-2 by Richard Newcomb, the *Stamford Mercury* proprietor. They were part of a property empire built up by Newcomb to dissipate Cecil influence

in the town. Rock Terrace (*ST, 27*) is comparable in scale to Rutland Terrace while Rock House is a huge Victorian Italianate villa built for Newcomb himself.

31. ALL SAINTS' BREWERY
All Saints' Street

An industrial site right in the heart of town. The brewery was built by William Edwards in the 1820s; many of the original buildings survive including the Brewery House on Scotgate. The brewery was taken over by Melbourn's in 1872 and their steam brewing equipment is still in place. Brewing ceased in 1974 and the building is now a museum operated by Samuel Smith of Tadcaster, Yorkshire.

32. MALTINGS/HUNT'S BREWERY
Water Street

Water Street was the main malting and brewing area of the town. Some mid 19th-century maltings buildings still survive off the south-west end of the street. Part of Hunt's Brewery can be found at the east end facing the river; the brewery opened in 1814 and closed in 1927. Welland House (No. 16) of 1834 was the home of Joseph Phillips, Stamford's principal brewer.

33. DANIEL LAMBERT'S GRAVE
St Martin's Churchyard
Off Barnack Road

When Daniel Lambert died in Stamford on 21 June 1809, aged 39, he was the heaviest man in Britain. He weighed almost 53 stone (336kg) and measured 3ft 11in around the leg and 9ft 4in around the waist. His gravestone is made of Swithland Slate, quarried just north of his home town of Leicester.

SURROUNDING AREA

1. ST MATTHEW'S CHURCH
NORMANTON, Rutland
6 miles west of Stamford

The church is remarkable mainly for its unique setting. It stands on an artificial spit jutting out into Rutland Water and appears to be slowly sinking into the waves. The Baroque tower was designed in 1826-9 by Thomas Cundy the younger and is based on Wren's St John's Church in Smith Square, London. The rest of the church is Neo-Classical of 1911.

2. BELVOIR CASTLE
BELVOIR, Leicestershire
22 miles north-west of Stamford

The original Belvoir Castle was built in the late 11th century by Robert de Todeni, whose family founded a hospital at Newstead just east of Stamford. The house was an important Royalist garrison during the Civil War. The present house was the brainchild of the 5th Duchess of Rutland and was designed by James Wyatt from 1801 until his death in 1813; however, the north and east wings were damaged by fire in 1816 and were remodelled by Sir John Thoroton. The house is spectacularly situated on a sudden hilltop and with its varied outline of towers, turrets and battlements, it is, as Pevsner says 'the *beau idéal* of the romantic castle'. Architecturally it is a Georgian interpretation of various medieval styles, especially the 13th century as found at Lincoln Cathedral. The house is open to the public. A few miles north is St Mary's Church at Bottesford which contains the splendid monuments of the Earls and Dukes of Rutland.

3. ELTON HALL
ELTON, Cambridgeshire
9 miles south of Stamford

Although the house was begun in the late 15th century, it is the 18th- and 19th- century alterations which now dominate. Classical, Gothick and Victorian Gothic features jostle with original 15th-century remains. The house is open to the public.

4. HOUSE OF CORRECTION
FOLKINGHAM, Lincolnshire
19 miles north of Stamford

An amazing building designed in 1825 by Stamford architect Bryan Browning. All that survives is the gatehouse-cum-governor's house. Pevsner compares it with Sanmicheli's town gates, Ledoux's toll gates and Vanbrugh. It is now owned by the Landmark Trust. See also *ST, 13*.

5. HARLAXTON MANOR
HARLAXTON, Lincolnshire
20 miles north-west of Stamford

The gargantuan scale of this immense house is simultaneously overwhelming and compelling. Pevsner says 'It must be seen to be believed. It is without any doubt the wildest and most fanciful mansion of the 1830s - High Victorian, one would be tempted to say, rather than early Victorian - and it has certain interiors again so gloriously and thickly Baroque that the 1830s seems an unbelievably early date.' This vast palace was built by Gregory Gregory, a bachelor from an old landed family. It was designed by Gregory and architects Anthony Salvin and William Burn and was built from 1831 to 1851. It is a unique fusion of Elizabethan (copied from Burghley House and elsewhere) and Baroque in the style of Vanbrugh's Blenheim. The approach along a straight drive, a mile in length, is stunning. The house is now owned by the University of Evansville, Indiana, U.S.A., and is open to the public on certain days.

6. STOKE ROCHFORD HALL
STOKE ROCHFORD, Lincolnshire
15 miles north of Stamford
This house was built in 1841-43 by Christopher Turner in response to Gregory Gregory's incredible house (*SA*, *5*). It was designed by William Burn, who worked at Harlaxton, and cost £60,000. The style uses an assortment of Elizabethan and Jacobean motifs. In the grounds is a 60ft obelisk in honour of Sir Isaac Newton. The house is now a conference centre and can be viewed from public footpaths.

7. THE ELMS (PRIORY SCHOOL) CLARE LODGE
WOTHORPE, Cambridgeshire
½ mile south-west of Stamford
Two large and eccentric mid 19th-century houses built by Stamford architect Edward Browning. The Elms was Browning's home and incorporates fragments of medieval architecture removed during church restorations. Clare Lodge is a bizarre Tudor-Gothic villa with a heavy wooden gable influenced by French vernacular architecture.

8. NEWSTEAD MILL
NEWSTEAD, Lincolnshire
1 mile east of Stamford
One of the largest water-powered mills in the county. It was built in *c*.1840 on the River Gwash to grind corn. It has recently been converted into flats.

9. WINDMILLS
Windmills were once a common sight around Stamford. The base of one survives off the A43 at Easton-on-the-Hill; another, with an onion-dome (ogee) top can be seen near Barnack. A complete example is visible from the A47 just east of Morcott (Rut.). A rare 8-sailer mill, dated 1830, can be visited at Heckington, near Sleaford, 30 miles to the north-east.

10. NENE VALLEY RAILWAY
STIBBINGTON, Cambridgeshire
7 miles south of Stamford
11. RUTLAND RAILWAY MUSEUM
Near COTTESMORE, Rutland
9 miles north-west of Stamford
Two very different steam railway museums. Nene Valley runs all the way to Peterborough and has locomotives and stock from over 9 countries. Rutland is a centre for industrial railways.

12. BIRTHPLACE OF JOHN CLARE
HELPSTON, Cambridgeshire
7 miles east of Stamford
John Clare, the poet, was born in this fenland village on 13 July 1793. In his youth he worked as a gardener at Burghley House and his first works were published with the help of a Stamford printer. He died in 1864 and was buried at Helpston.

20TH CENTURY
TOWARDS EQUALITY/ TOURIST & RETIREMENT TOWN
STAMFORD

1. Nos. 23-24 HIGH STREET
This huge Baroque-style department store was built in 1904 by the drapery firm of Oates and Musson; the two-storey plate glass windows must have been a daring novelty in Stamford at the time. The upper windows are inspired by No. 19 St George's Square of 1674 (*see* C17*ST*, *10*). Unfortunately the original roof pediments were not rebuilt after a fire in 1965.

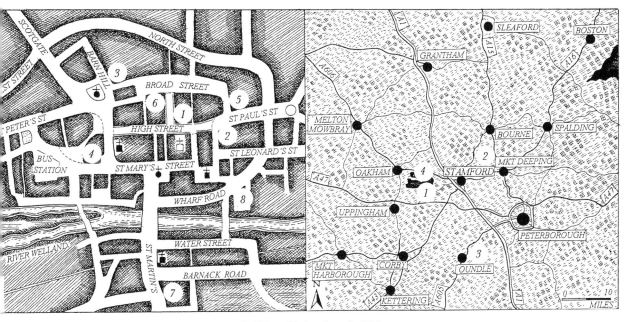

Above: *Buildings & sites from the 20th century*

2. No. 41 HIGH STREET

In 1909, the Peterborough Co-operative Society dismantled an 18th-century building on this site and incorporated its basic form (using original fragments) into a new, larger department store. The 2 bays down St Paul's Street are in a contrasting Tudoresque style. The architects were Townsend and Fordham of Peterborough. The dull sub-Georgian south range was built in *c.*1966.

3. CROWN HOTEL
All Saints' Place

The last building in the town to be constructed from Wittering Pendle stone. The hotel was rebuilt in *c.*1908. The odd bowed and canted window bays echo the design of the original hotel building.

4. LONDON INN
St John's Street

5. HALF MOON INN
St Paul's Street

Two 17th-century vernacular style buildings erected in the late 1930s. The Half Moon was rebuilt in 1938 to designs by H. F. Traylen. The London Inn, dating from 1939-40, is more accomplished and has four canted and gabled window bays. It was rebuilt as the first part of an aborted traffic scheme which involved widening St John's Street and building a relief road across the meadows and through Sheepmarket.

6. CENTRAL CINEMA
Broad Street

The cinema was rebuilt in 1938 following a devastating fire. It was designed by the famous cinema architect George Coles of London, and mixes typical 1930s motifs, such as the tiled rotunda entrance hall with its Egyptian-style columns, with more conservative neo-Georgian elements. In 1993-4, the cinema was converted into a pub and shop units.

7. No. 31 HIGH STREET ST MARTIN'S

An accomplished neo-Georgian infill building designed in 1936 by C. B. Metcalfe for Stamford High School. No. 34 is also neo-Georgian but dates from 1964; it was designed by Stamford architect W. J. Hemmings.

8. No. 24 WHARF ROAD

The house where Malcolm Sargent, the famous musician and conductor, grew up. Sargent was born in 1895 and lived here until he was 18. He died in 1967 and is buried in Stamford Cemetery off Little Casterton Road.

SURROUNDING AREA

1. PASTURES HOUSE
NORTH LUFFENHAM, Rutland
8 miles west of Stamford

At the end of the village on the road to Morcott is a delightful house by C. F. A. Voysey, built in 1901 for Miss G. Conant. The style is archetypal Voysey with gables, mullioned windows and a superb semi-circular porch-entrance. This type of porch was later copied by suburban house builders throughout the country. Good Voysey-style houses can be found in Stamford at Nos. 39-41 Casterton Road and in Ryhall Road.

2. GREATFORD, *Lincolnshire*
5 miles north-east of Stamford

A village full of strange follies: carved obelisks, mushrooms, giant coronets, elephants and Norman basins are scattered everywhere. They were commissioned in the 1930s by Major Fitzwilliam of Greatford Hall.

3. ASHTON, *Northamptonshire*
Near Oundle, 15 miles south of Stamford

A model thatched estate village built in 1900 by Hon. Charles Rothschild, 2nd son of 1st Lord Rothschild. It was designed by an architect called Hackvale. Ashton is the host of the annual World Conker Championships.

4. RUTLAND WATER
Near EMPINGHAM, Rutland
5 miles west of Stamford

Rutland Water is the size of Lake Windermere and is one of the largest man-made lakes in Europe. It was constructed in the early 1970s. It is supplied with water pumped from the Welland and Nene rivers.

FURTHER READING

It is not my intention here to give a comprehensive bibliography; *Stamford Then and Now* by Martin Smith has a full Stamford book list. Instead, I offer a selective guide to further reading.

For the early history of the town see *East Midlands in the Early Middle Ages* by Pauline Stafford (Leicester, 1985); 'Stamford: the development of an Anglo-Scandinavian Borough' by David. R. Roffe and Christine M. Mahany in *Anglo-Norman Studies 5: Proceedings of Battle Conference 1982* (Bury St Edmunds, 1983); 'Stamford and the Norman Conquest' by the same authors in *Lincolnshire History and Archaeology*, 21 (1986); *Stamford Castle and Town* by Christine M. Mahany (Stamford, 1978); *Excavations in Stamford, Lincolnshire 1963-1969* by Christine M. Mahany, Alan Burchard and Gavin Simpson (London, 1982); *Excavations at Stamford Castle 1971-1976* by Christine M. Mahany (CBA monograph, forthcoming); 'Walter Dragun's Town? Lord and Burghal Community in Thirteenth Century Stamford' by David R. Roffe in *Lincolnshire History and Archaeology* (1988) pp.43-46 and *Stamford in the Thirteenth Century: Two Inquisitions from the Reign of Edward I* by David R. Roffe (Stamford, 1994). Francis Peck's *Antiquarian Annals of Stamford* (London, 1727; reprinted, Wakefield, 1979) has a lot of information on the medieval period but use the reprint as it has an index; also bear in mind that much of the early history is erroneous. For medieval architecture look at *The Medieval Buildings of Stamford* by Alan Rogers and the Stamford Survey Group (Nottingham, 1970); *The Religious Foundations of Medieval Stamford* by John S. Hartley and Alan Rogers (Nottingham, 1974); *The Town of Stamford* by the Royal Commission on the Historical Monuments of England (London, 1977) which is a detailed inventory of all buildings erected before 1850 and *Stamford Then and Now* by Martin Smith (Stamford, 1992) which is a unique study of architectural change in the town. *The Stones of Stamford* by A. S. Ireson (Stamford, 1986) is an excellent guide to building materials.

For later centuries look at *The Making of Stamford* edited by Alan Rogers (Leicester, 1965) which is a collection of essays on the development of the town; *Stamford and the Civil War* by Christopher Davies (Stamford, 1992); *A Family Affair: Stamford and the Cecils 1650-1900* by E. C. Till (Rugby, 1990) and *The Survey and the Antiquities of the Towne of Stamford* (Stamford, 1646; reprint, 1717) by Richard Butcher which is the first history of the town and contains interesting contemporary information. *The Antiquities of Stamford and St Martin's* by William Harrod (Stamford, 1785) has useful information on the 18th century as does John Drakard's *History of Stamford* (Stamford, 1822) which is heavily political. For industrial history look at *Stamford - an Industrial History* by N. C. Birch (Lincolnshire Archaeology Group, 1972); *A Century of Stamford Coachbuilding* by Michael Key (Stamford, 1990) and *Pick of Stamford: a History of the Pick Motor Company Ltd.* by the same author (Stamford, 1994); *Great Northern Branch Lines to Stamford* by John Rhodes (Boston, 1988) and *The Stamford and Essendine Railway* by D. L. Franks (Leeds, 1971). For the 19th century see George Burton's *Chronology of Stamford* (Stamford, 1846); A. J. Waterfield's *Annals of Stamford* (Stamford, 1887) and copies of the *Stamford Mercury*. For 20th century see *Ninety Years of Cinema in Stamford* by Brian Hornsey (Stamford, 1990); *Stamford and the Great War* by W. F. Marwick (Stamford, c.1919) and *Stamford Remembered* and *Stamford Memories* by Betty Clark (Stamford, 1988, 1989).

For Stamford folklore see *The Myths and Legends of Stamford in Lincolnshire* by Martin Smith (Stamford, 1991) which contains information on the Stamford 'university', bull-running, Daniel Lambert and William Stukeley.

INDEX

Normal numerals refer to main text; *italic* numerals refer to Gazetteer and **bold** numerals refer to photographs and maps. The index has several major groupings: Almshouses; Architects; Battles; Bridges; Building Materials; Castles; Churches & Chapels; Country Houses; Industry, Crafts & Trade; Inns; Kings & Queens; Museums; Newspapers; Parliament; Politics; Religious Houses; Religious Sects; Rivers; Roads; Schools; Shops; Streets; Transport and Wars. Lack of space means that only important entries are cross referenced.